C000081883

THE
ULTIMATE
CABIN CREW
INTERVIEW
Q & A
BOOK

Lauren Matthews

YOURS TO HAVE AND TO HOLD
BUT NOT TO COPY

First edition 2006

ISBN   978-0-9552818-4-6

A catalogue record for this book is available from the British Library.

Published 2006 in the United Kingdom by CE Publishing

INTRODUCTION

The Ultimate Cabin Crew Interview Q&A Book is unlike any other book available...

In this book, you'll get hundreds of the toughest, sneakiest and, meanest questions that recruiters love to throw at you and with each question will be 1 or 2 detailed sample answers, which can be adapted and customised to your individual circumstances.

You will discover precisely what the interviewers want to hear and then rehearse your script in advance.

Remember: A job interview is a screen test, an act. Getting hired depends almost completely on the actor factor. If you know your lines and perfect your delivery you'll get hired. If you don't, you won't.

Because interviews are so predictable, they're controllable. Only the places and faces change – not the words. And you can have them all embedded in your subconscious, ready for instant replay at the drop of an interview.

CONTENTS

QUESTIONS & ANSWERS

Cabin crew interview questions are fairly unique in that the questioning tends to focus almost exclusively on personal qualities. As a result, there are no definite right or wrong answers, just more appropriate answers and better forms of expression.

It is important to have examples ready, to back up any statements made. For example "I enjoy providing customer care" may be investigated with the follow up: "When have you provided good customer care?" or perhaps a statement like "I appreciate there are times when a crew member has to remain calm under pressure" would be followed with the question "When have you experienced a pressured situation?"

In the following pages, I have listed various interview questions, followed by examples of effective ways to answering each of them in a detailed, yet concise manner. Whilst the answers provided are based around an individual whose career is in hairdressing, each of the answers may be adapted to suit your individual circumstance.

When a question that is asked is based around a personal experience you have encountered, try to keep to the following guidelines when formulating your answers...

- Choose an experience that demonstrates an interaction that resulted in a positive experience for all concerned
- Try to keep your answers detailed yet concise
- Begin by briefly stating what happened
- Go on to describe what you did and how you dealt with the situation
- Briefly describe your feelings and concerns when you were faced with the situation and how the other person may have also felt

- Describe the outcome
- Explain how your actions affected the other person/outcome
- Then state what you learned from the experience

Below is a good example of an answer which covers each of these points...

WHAT HAPPENED

"I recently experienced a situation with a client who was having relationship problems and who became very emotional."

HOW THE CLIENT MAY HAVE FELT

"I could sense that she was feeling very depressed and I tried to think of what I could do to help. "

WHAT I DID

"I gave her chance to talk while I listened. This seemed to calm her down. Once I heard her story, I showed empathy and concern for her situation whilst not getting too involved. "

HOW I FELT

"It was a difficult situation and felt compassion for the client's situation. It was a real struggle to maintain my poised mask, but I managed to keep my emotions under control."

POSITIVE OUTCOME AND HOW MY ACTIONS AFFECTED THE CLIENT/OUTCOME

"As a result of my listening and showing concern, the client began seeing her situation more clearly and became much more positive. Consequently, she was able to calmly discuss her feelings with her partner and work through their problems. She later thanked me for listening and told me I was very caring and professional. It made me feel good that I was able to make such a big difference. She's now a regular client of mine."

WHAT I LEARNED FROM THIS EXPERIENCE

"From this experience, I learned that just listening can be providing good customer care and ultimately change someone's future to a more positive one."

Do your best to have several positive experiences prepared before the interview and make sure the experiences are true.

Please remember...

The answers provided on the following pages are designed to be used as a guide to assist you in formulating your own answers and should not be copied in their entirety.

BACKGROUND

Personal Details

Outside Interests

Education & Training

Work Experience & Employment History

Professional Knowledge & Experience

These kinds of questions draw from personal experience, and are fairly easy to answer, so they are often used to settle candidates into an interview. Selectors also use background questions as a reference point from which to introduce the more role-specific questions.

Recruiters are likely to probe with follow up questions if they think there are revealing aspects about qualities they wish to explore (or potential problems, such as long/frequent periods of sickness).

Tip: Be positive about the work you do, and about your outside interests. Negative or pessimistic attitudes are unlikely to advance your cause! Also, if you consider the kind of qualities selectors are trying to identify, you will be better able to phrase your replies to make the most favourable impression.

PERSONAL DETAILS

HOW MUCH TIME DO YOU SPEND WITH YOUR FAMILY?

Whilst my family are important to me and I like to be there for them when they need me, I have a responsibility to my work and they understand and accept the commitment I have made. So I spend my time accordingly.

WHAT IS YOUR MARITAL STATUS/DO YOU PLAN TO HAVE CHILDREN/GET MARRIED?

I am presently single. I do have plans to get married and have children, but those plans are for the future. I have certain career goals that I would like to achieve first.

DO YOU SMOKE?

No.

HAVE YOU EVER SMOKED?

Yes. I gave it up in the spring of 2003

DO YOU CONSIDER YOURSELF A SOCIAL DRINKER?

I don't drink alcohol but I don't have a problem with people who do.

WHEN WAS YOUR LAST PHYSICAL EXAMINATION?

It was last year, and my health was excellent.

DO YOU FEEL APPEARANCE IS IMPORTANT?

Yes, to a certain extent. Appearance is important in the sense that you should be neat, clean and tidy. Your appearance contributes to whether people will have the confidence in you – and the ability to inspire confidence is a great asset.

Whilst appearance is an important factor, so is tone of voice, manner, and behaviour important.

DO YOU HOLD A VALID DRIVING LICENCE?

Yes; I have a valid licence.

HAVE YOU EVER BEEN CONVICTED OF A DRIVING OFFENCE?

No, I always drive carefully.

HOW WOULD THE JOB IMPACT YOUR FAMILY/HOME LIFE?

The impact would not be great, if any as I can keep in contact easily through the internet and using the telephone.

WHAT DO YOUR FAMILY THINK ABOUT YOU APPLYING FOR THIS POSITION/YOUR CHOSEN CAREER?

My family understand the decision I have made and support me 100%.

THIS POSITION REQUIRES LONG HOURS, WILL THIS BE A PROBLEM FOR YOUR SOCIAL/FAMILY LIFE?

My career plays an important part of my life. My family and friends realise and appreciate the fact and are very flexible with my schedule. They support me 100 percent.

OUTSIDE INTERESTS

WHAT HOBBIES AND INTERESTS DO YOU HAVE/WHAT DO YOU DO WITH YOUR SPARE TIME?

I don't get a lot of time to indulge myself, but I always make a point to include myself in sporting activities. I regularly participate in cardiovascular exercise, such as cycling, swimming, running and yoga. Occasionally when I am able, I also enjoy badminton and aerobics.

I also enjoy an active social life, and enjoy reading, cooking and travelling.

WHAT DO YOU DO TO RELAX AFTER A HARD DAY?

After a hard day, I either go for a swim, a sauna or perform my yoga and relaxation routines to make a break from the environment and help me unwind.

DO YOU PREFER TEAM SPORTS OR INDIVIDUAL ONES?

I don't differentiate between team and individual sports. Both kinds have their strong points; teamwork and team spirit on one hand and individual strength and self-reliance on the other. To me, the most important aspects of sport are achievement and hard work, so I try to mix both, if possible.

WHAT IS YOUR ENERGY LEVEL LIKE/WHERE DO YOU GET YOUR ENERGY FROM?

My energy levels are on top form; working freelance isn't possible unless you have plenty of energy. To keep them that way; I routinely involve myself in cardiovascular exercise. If you have too much energy, cardiovascular exercise uses some of it up. If I have too little it stimulates the body's systems and finds you some.

YOUR INTERESTS APPEAR RATHER SOLITARY, CYCLING, SWIMMING, RUNNING, READING, YOGA ETC. HOW DO YOU THINK THIS REFLECTS YOUR PERSONALITY?

I like to think they suggest a sense of balance. In my work I spend a lot of time with clients and I have an active social life outside of work, so it can be good to relax sometimes and do something completely different. In any case, these activities, I quite often do with company.

WHICH IS YOUR FAVOURITE ACTIVITY/WHAT SATISFACTION DO YOU GET FROM YOUR INTERESTS?

I don't have a favourite, as such. This is because each of the activities I participate in requires or provides something different, and therefore, each activity is equally enjoyable in their own ways.

I particularly enjoy cycling, swimming, yoga, badminton, and rock climbing. These activities keep me in top physical condition and make me more effective in everything I do.

WHAT HAVE YOU ACHIEVED THROUGH YOUR INTERESTS?

Apart from the obvious benefits, such as fitness and stamina, I have achieved a healthier, stress free lifestyle. My interests have also helped me develop my team spirit and ability to work with others towards a common goal.

HOW OFTEN DO YOU DO YOGA/ WHAT SKILLS/QUALITIES ARE REQUIRED/WHAT DO YOU LIKE ABOUT IT?

I try to perform yoga stretches on a daily basis at home. I enjoy yoga because is very convenient to perform, in terms of time and space and is a great way to relax, relieve stress and gain flexibility. It also requires commitment, mental discipline and high concentration

HOW OFTEN DO YOU PLAY BADMINTON/ WHAT SKILLS/QUALITIES ARE REQUIRED/WHAT DO YOU LIKE ABOUT IT?

I play badminton as often as possible, when the opportunity presents itself. However, I do not have as much time as I would like to indulge myself fully. I enjoy the friendly competition and it is a great way to relieve stress and keep fit.

EDUCATION AND TRAINING

School

WHY DIDN'T YOU DO BETTER IN YOUR EXAMS?

My results were above average, as with most other people, if I could do it again, my grades would be much higher. I'd not only work harder, but I've also learned a lot since then.

WHAT WERE YOUR FAVOURITE SUBJECTS?

I always felt great interest towards Geography; I am fascinated by the changing world. I particularly enjoyed learning about different continents – terrains, cultures, the environments, the landscapes etc...

WHAT SUBJECTS GAVE YOU THE MOST DIFFICULTY?

I never had a great deal of knowledge about science, but I forced myself to study hard so I managed to achieve above average results.

WHAT SUBJECTS WERE THE EASIEST FOR YOU?

I wouldn't say that any of the subjects were easy, as they all required hard work. However, because I have a natural creative ability, Art and Design was the one I found to be the least difficult. I felt a great deal of pleasure from those lessons and my exam results were outstanding.

I SEE YOU STUDIED FRENCH AT SCHOOL, WHAT IS YOUR FLUENCY?

I studied French in high school and found the language very interesting. I am not as fluent as I once was, I understand a lot of the basics, such as greetings, introducing myself, the alphabet and numbers 1 -100 etc. I would welcome the opportunity to increase my fluency.

WHY DIDN'T YOU STAY ON AT SCHOOL OR CONTINUE FULL TIME EDUCATION/ DO YOU FEEL YOU MADE THE RIGHT CHOICE?

I did consider continuing full time education, but I had really enjoyed my work experience at Any Hair Salon, and wanted to start on work I enjoyed as soon as possible, it wasn't long before I realised I had made the right choice.

Or

I wanted to continue full time education, but personal circumstances meant that I needed to earn a living rather than run up debts studying. Education comes from places other than college.

Further Education and Training

TELL US ABOUT YOUR FURTHER EDUCATION AND TRAINING/WHAT STEPS HAVE YOU TAKEN TO INCREASE YOUR SKILLS AND EXPERIENCE?

Since leaving school I have used every opportunity to expand my knowledge and acquire further skills. Whilst working at Any Hair Salon, I studied part time to achieve my NVQ levels 1, 2 and 3 in hairdressing. During this time, I also completed a creative cutting course, alongside the comprehensive on-the-job training I received through the salon,

I also educate myself informally through reading journals and reviewing self help techniques in books; and I subscribe to trade magazines. So I have continued to learn and grow.

WHAT TRADE MAGAZINES DO YOU SUBSCRIBE TO/WHAT JOURNALS DO YOU READ?

Hairdressers Journal International, Estetica/Cutting Edge, Creative Head, Professional Beauty and Black Beauty Hair.

WHAT AREAS OF SELF DEVELOPMENT DO YOU STUDY THROUGH BOOKS?

Delivering customer care, dealing with difficult situations/complaints, stress management, etc.

WHAT DO YOU DO TO IMPROVE YOURSELF?

I don't think a day has passed in my career that I didn't improve my skills to some extent. I've always found that if you want to learn, there's plenty to be picked up every day.

As a hairstylist the learning and development process never ends. Not only are you developing your practical skills but also your social skills.

Current and Future Development

WHAT ARE YOUR EDUCATIONAL GOALS FOR THE FUTURE/ WHAT DO YOU PLAN TO DO TO IMPROVE YOURSELF/WHAT AREA OF YOUR SKILLS AND/OR DEVELOPMENT WOULD YOU LIKE TO IMPROVE ON?

Self improvement plays an important part in my life, and I'll continue developing myself every day, both on the job and off. I think likely that I will work on improving my language, management and interpersonal skills further.

Or

Although I consider my ability to work well with people, to motivate them and communicate with them effectively as one of the my most important assets, I try constantly to keep improving those skills even further.

General

DO YOU FEEL YOU'RE EDUCATION AND TRAINING PREPARED YOU WELL FOR THE CHALLENGES IN THE WORK FORCE?

My education and training gave me a solid foundation on which I built my knowledge base and gave me the confidence to face the future challenges. To achieve good results at school I had to work hard, set my goals and do my best to achieve them. The same principles apply in the work force. The problem-solving and goal-setting skills that I acquired have helped me a lot throughout my career.

HOW HAS YOUR EDUCATION PREPARED YOU FOR THE ROLE OF CABIN CREW?

This position requires knowledge and skills that I acquired through my education and training, such as dealing with customers, working as part of a team and selling products/services. Many of the subjects I studied at school are also directly related to the job such as English, Geography and Mathematics, yet what school really taught me that has helped throughout my career and will prove very useful to this position was how to solve problems, how to apply myself, and how to set a goal and achieve it.

DO YOU THINK GRADES SHOULD BE CONSIDERED BY NEW EMPLOYERS?

Of course, an employer should take everything into consideration, and along with grades will be an evaluation of willingness and manageability, an understanding of how business works, and actual work experience. Combined, such experience and professional skills can be more valuable than grades alone.

WHAT IS YOUR OPINION OF THE IMPORTANCE OF TRAINING AND DEVELOPMENT?

Effective training and development is absolutely necessary in order to improve efficiency and readiness for the work force.

I SEE YOU ARE CURRENTLY LEARNING SPANISH, WHAT IS YOUR LEVEL OF FLUENCY?

As the language is very similar to French, I am picking it up fairly quickly, however, I have only recently began learning the language. Hopefully, in the next few months I should gain a basic level of reading, writing and speaking.

WORK EXPERIENCE AND EMPLOYMENT HISTORY

Previous Employers

HOW WOULD YOU EVALUATE ANY HAIR SALON /WAS IT A GOOD SALON TO WORK FOR/ WHAT DID YOU LIKE ABOUT THE ENVIRONMENT?

I can say only good things about Any Hair Salon. There was always a vibrant atmosphere, the people were great – they were very talented and fantastically professional. There were no arbitrary lines between seniority and staff, but rather a team of skilled professionals all working together. I was given all the opportunities that were available and received more hands on training and attention than I could ever have hoped for.

WHY DID YOU CHOOSE ANY HAIR SALON?

Initially, I chose Any Hair Salon because of the familiarity after having carried out two weeks of work experience within the salon whilst I was at school. However, I also chose the salon in particular because of its good reputation and practicality and having been a customer on several occasions, I knew it was the salon I wanted to work for. The salon had an atmosphere all of its own and it wasn't long before I realised I had made the right choice.

WHAT REPUTATION DID THE SALON HAVE/WHAT HAD YOU HEARD ABOUT THE SALON?

They had a reputation for being a very likeable place - Great service, talented workers, good customer care, vibrant atmosphere.

WHAT DID YOU WISH YOU KNEW ABOUT THE SALON BEFORE YOU STARTED?

I had done work experience within the salon and had also been a customer on more than one occasion, because of this, everything that I wanted or needed to know, I already knew.

WHAT COULD ANY HAIR SALON HAVE DONE BETTER?

As an employer, they were fine and I have no complaints. As for the service and customer care, I don't think we could have done better. There was always a vibrant atmosphere, the people were great – they were very talented and fantastically professional.

IF PROBED FURTHER

I really can't think of anything that could have been improved. Anything that could have been improved had already been done.

Or

Any Hair Salon never given me anything to complain about. I knew that it was a wonderful salon.

WHY DID YOU STAY WITH THE SAME EMPLOYER FOR SO LONG?

I was there for several years, but in a variety of different roles so it felt as though I was undergoing frequent changes without actually changing employer.

Co-workers

TELL US ABOUT YOUR LAST WORK GROUP/DID YOU GET ALONG WITH YOUR CO WORKERS?

My colleagues at Any Hair Salon were good natured but serious about work. There were only 8 of us in the team upon leaving (including myself and the manager), which made for a very relaxed atmosphere. We all became close and worked well as a team. I enjoyed the time I spent with them.

DID BEING CLOSE CAUSE PROBLEMS DURING WORK?

No, there were no problems. We worked very professionally together.

TELL US ABOUT YOUR PREVIOUS SUPERIORS?

From the time I began working at Any Hair Salon, my superiors took a sincere interest in my work, under their guidance, I grew personally and professionally.

My manager was a good role model and motivator. We had a very productive relationship and got along really well. She taught me many necessary skills and work methods and provided constant motivation and encouragement for my efforts. She was always full of good advice in a crisis and very generous with her time if anyone needed consoling. She could always make people laugh and was confident enough to be able to make fun of herself and her own mistakes.

I consider myself very fortunate to have had her by my side early in my career, as a supervisor, teacher and remarkable person. She served as a role model for me and helped me develop my leadership and interpersonal skills.

My supervisor was a firm, fair and consistent leader, who expected a lot from us and taught us to expect a lot from ourselves. There was always a feeling of mutual trust and respect and as a result she earned the loyalty and respect of the entire team, including myself. She often came and asked about the work progress and to see if we needed any help, though she didn't over manage, but gave us the opportunity to use all of our initiative and skill to solve problems and get things done.

I liked them as people, respected them professionally, and appreciated their guidance. I would say that we respected each other's individual skills and personal qualities.

HOW DID YOUR SUPERIORS GET THE BEST OUT OF YOU?
My superiors always got superior effort and performance, but by treating me like a human being and giving me the same personal respect with which they liked to be treated themselves was definitely an added motivator.

WHAT DID YOU DISLIKE ABOUT YOUR SUPERIORS? HOW COULD YOUR SUPERIORS HAVE DONE A BETTER JOB?
You know, I've never thought of our relationship in terms of like or dislike. I've always thought our role was to get along together and get the job done. I have always had the highest respect for my superiors and they couldn't have done a better job.

SURELY THERE MUST HAVE BEEN SOMETHING YOU DISLIKED ABOUT THEM

I'm lucky to have had very supportive superiors who were good at their jobs and very easy to work with. I honestly can't think of anything that I disliked or could have been improved.

(No matter how much the recruiters probe, don't be drawn into divulging criticism – stick to your guns)

Present Employment

TELL US ABOUT YOUR CURRENT JOB/WHAT ARE YOUR DUTIES?

Working freelance, I have a broad range of responsibilities. In addition to the hairdressing service, I am also responsible for holding consultations, attending to telephone enquiries and phasing appointments, advising clients on suitable styles and treatments and giving aftercare advice. I am also responsible for the day to day running of the business, such as, checking, ordering, and maintaining stock, calculating client bills and collecting payments, providing a point of sale for retail goods, keeping up to date accounts, advertising, establishing and maintaining relationships with clients, analysing and responding to feedback, and process improvement.

WHAT DO YOU LIKE ABOUT YOUR CURRENT JOB?

I like everything about my current job. I don't think I'd be able to really excel if I weren't truly interested in the work, or if I were merely motivated by its financial rewards.

Rather than pick out little details of the routine work, here are three general things. First, customer satisfaction, seeing the clients face glow with happiness when their hair has been transformed, it's very satisfying and drives me to do better. Second, I like constant interaction with people; it has enabled me to strengthen my communication and customer care skills.

And finally, I enjoy being creative with hair, and finding new ways to please the customer.

WHAT HAVE YOU ENJOYED MOST ABOUT WORKING FREELANCE/YOUR CURRENT JOB?

I enjoy the freedom, identity and status. I have the freedom to set my own goals and work to my own schedule. I have control over the products I use and can plan and use my time more effectively. I also enjoy the feeling of pride when I say goodbye to another satisfied client.

IF YOU GET THIS JOB, YOU WILL NOT HAVE THE FREEDOM TO WORK TO YOUR OWN SCHEDULE, IS THIS GOING TO BE A PROBLEM?

No, this will not be a problem as my current job requires me to be very flexible. So if I was to get this job, I would naturally adapt.

WHAT PARTICULAR ASPECT OF YOUR JOB DO YOU FIND MOST REWARDING/WHAT IS YOUR FAVOURITE PART OF THE JOB?

The most rewarding aspect of my job is definitely seeing the clients face glow with happiness when their hair has been transformed, it's very satisfying and makes me proud to see what I have done.

WHAT DO YOU DISLIKE ABOUT YOUR CURRENT JOB/WHAT IS THE WORST PART OF THE JOB?

I really like this work, so I honestly can't think of any major dislikes. I guess my answer will have to come under the category or nuisances. The biggest nuisance is the paperwork that seems to slow down the action. I realise the importance of documentation, and I cooperatively fill out the forms. But I'm always looking for efficiencies in that area that will get me out in front of the customer where I belong.

WHAT HAVE YOU ENJOYED LEAST ABOUT WORKING FREELANCE/YOUR CURRENT JOB?

It is exciting working freelance and I have built up a substantial base of satisfied customers, however, the drawback to working freelance is the lack of security. I don't know what the future holds and sometimes that is a frightening concept. Although no job is secure nowadays, I would prefer to have a situation where I can follow a clear career path. I think even more significantly, I actually miss working with other people and having colleagues to share ideas with. I like working in a team environment.

WHICH PARTICULAR ASPECT OF YOUR WORK DO YOU FIND MOST FRUSTRATING?

That's an interesting question, because I am, generally speaking, a tolerant person. However, slow periods can be sources of frustration, but at times like that, I put more effort into advertising and establishing new clientele. That way, the slow periods don't last long.

WHAT MADE YOU DECIDE TO GO FREELANCE/WHY NOT STAY AT ANY HAIR SALON OR MOVE TO ANOTHER SALON?

I liked the fact that working freelance would require me to use all of my initiative and skills to solve problems and get things done. I also like the fact that working freelance would mean more opportunity to work the hours I chose, and that would give me the time to work on advancing my career in the airline industry.

WHY DO YOU WANT TO LEAVE YOUR CURRENT WORK?

Being cabin crew is something I have always wanted to do and I am now at a point in my life where I am prepared to make the career and lifestyle change and I want to take advantage of that opportunity.

IN WHAT WAYS ARE YOU PREPARED FOR THE CAREER AND LIFESTYLE CHANGE?

I am prepared in many ways; I am prepared in my attitude – maturity, enthusiasm, etc. I am prepared in my life – financially able; don't have big commitments, etc. And I have the required skills and experience – customer care, teamwork, etc.

DESCRIBE A TYPICAL DAY/WEEK/WHAT DO YOU SPEND MOST OF YOUR TIME DOING/HOW MANY HOURS A WEEK DO YOU FIND NECESSARY TO GET YOUR WORK DONE?

My work load varies considerably from day to day and week to week because I work on demand. When work comes in, the majority of my time is spent on putting whatever effort is required into getting the work completed. The rest of my time is spent on establishing and maintaining effective relationships with clients, collecting supplies, analysing and responding to feedback, advertising and book keeping. Further than that, it's very hard to say exactly what else I might be doing as I try to be responsive to demand.

WHY ARE YOU DISSATISFIED WITH YOUR CURRENT JOB?

I'm not dissatisfied with my job, in many ways I am very happy where I am. I'm not looking around actively, but there are only so many extraordinary opportunities that come along in this life and this is one of them. The post you are filling calls for the skills I have and offers the scope I want.

WHAT SPECIFIC STRENGTHS DID YOU BRING TO YOUR CURRENT JOB THAT MADE YOU PARTICULARLY EFFECTIVE?

My extensive knowledge and experience in hairdressing, coupled with my excellent customer care, and track record for accomplishment and dependability where my greatest assets, this along with the superior quality of my work and my reasonable prices enabled me to increase my customer base dramatically.

IN WHAT AREAS OF YOUR CURRENT WORK ARE YOU STRONGEST?

I am sure it is dealing with people – my interpersonal skills are very good and I pride myself on being able to build rapport quickly with new people. I think my professional attitude and common sense approach goes down well with clients and I have always received positive feedback with regards to follow through.

Additionally, I am good at what I do. I have a natural flair for design, good judgement and am good at coming up with new ideas.

On top of those reasons, I am really enthusiastic about my work and I put a great deal of energy into it.

IN WHAT AREAS OF YOUR CURRENT WORK ARE YOU WEAKEST?

I don't have any major weaknesses that interfere with how I do my work. The only area which can always be improved is the way to run a successful business. I have gained a great deal of business knowledge and experience during my freelancing career, such as time management, problem solving, book keeping, etc, but I feel that you can never be too good or should ever stop trying to polish your business skills.

HOW DO YOU DEFINE DOING A GOOD JOB IN YOUR PROFESSION?

A good job in my profession is the same as doing a good job in any profession, and that is giving satisfaction and impeccable service to the client, who is always the final judge of the service. A good job also means one I'm proud of, that gives me a sense of achievement and internal satisfaction, and is in line with my professional reputation.

WHY DO YOU THINK YOU HAVE SUCCEEDED AT WORKING FREELANCE?

No two clients are alike, and I feel that my secret to my success is making them feel that they get individual service created for their individual needs. Second, I place strong emphasis on quality, so my work is consistently exceptional; this combined with my reasonable prices has enabled me to increase my customer base dramatically. Third, I have mastered many important business skills that bring success, such as self motivation, time management, and problem solving.

And finally, I have worked hard and committed myself. It required lots of energy but I always give 100%

HOW COULD YOU HAVE IMPROVED YOUR PROGRESS/WHAT ARE SOME OF THE THINGS YOU COULD HAVE DONE TO BE MORE SUCCESSFUL?

I could have improved my progress by hiring a member of staff, and therefore increasing the range of services and clientele. However, I considered this not to be constructive because I knew that I wanted to advance my career as cabin crew.

Other than that, I don't know what to add. I've always given it my best shot.

IF YOU KNEW YOU WANTED TO ADVANCE YOUR CAREER AS CABIN CREW, WHY DID YOU GO FREELANCE AND NOT TRY FOR CABIN CREW WHEN YOU LEFT ANY HAIR SALON?

Before I advanced my career as cabin crew, I wanted to do some research into airlines that I would be interested in working for; working freelance allowed me the time and flexibility to do this.

WHAT CHARACTERISTICS (PERSONAL QUALITIES AND SKILLS) ARE NECESSARY FOR SUCCESS WORKING FREELANCE?

Working freelance, you have to be a self starter, spotting opportunities and acting on your own initiative without the support of others. You have to be self sufficient, drawing deeply on your experience and character. You need to be friendly, polite and able to talk to customers easily. You'll also need to anticipate your customer's needs and find innovative ways to get around various challenges that business life will throw at you, and be able to keep a cool head in a crisis.

WHAT CHARACTERISTICS (PERSONAL QUALITIES AND SKILLS) ARE NECESSARY FOR SUCCESS WORKING AS A HAIRDRESSER?

As it is a personal service in which the customer's satisfaction is the key to success, you need to be friendly, polite and able to talk to customers easily. You should work quickly and well with your hands, doing detailed work. A creative, artistic sense and an eye for colour and form is needed, along with an interest in fashion. Self-presentation is important so you should also be well groomed. You also need to be fit and able to stand for long periods.

HOW WOULD YOU COMPARE THE QUALITY OF YOUR WORK TO YOUR COMPETITORS/OTHER HAIRDRESSERS?

The quality of my work is to the same standard, if not better than that of my competitors. I take great pride in the quality of work I produce, and to further ensure quality I keep up to date with latest trends and fashions through subscribing to hairdressing journals.

I've always met or exceeded expectations.

HOW WOULD YOU COMPARE THE QUANTITY OF YOUR WORK TO YOUR COMPETITORS/OTHER HAIRDRESSERS?

Like the quality of the work I've produced, the overall quantity of my work has generally exceeded expectations. I set my pace according to what I can manage and what is required, and I always try to beat the clock and my own record. Due to my high energy and ability to find the fastest, most efficient way to get the work done, I'm able to keep increasing my output while maintaining quality.

HOW DO YOU MAINTAIN YOUR INTEREST IN YOUR WORK?

Quite easily; when I see the clients face glow with happiness when their hair is transformed, it's very satisfying and makes the hard work worth it. Also, because no two clients are the same and each requires something different, this makes the work much more interesting as I am able to utilise my creative ability.

WHAT HAVE YOU DONE TO MAKE YOUR WORK MORE EFFECTIVE?

To make my work more effective, I record and monitor everything I do. It ensures that I run a very professional business which is well disciplined and effective.

Details such as distance to a client's home (written in mileage), along with any factors that limited or affected the service with the client are recorded. From this data, I can identify better ways of doing things in terms of saving time and money, as a result of which I can focus more effort and energy on producing results and increasing profits.

WHAT HAVE YOU DONE TO MAKE YOUR WORK MORE CHALLENGING?

I usually set myself goals to try and push myself that bit further. However, my work is challenging enough without the need to create challenges.

WHAT HAVE YOU DONE TO MAKE YOUR WORK MORE INTERESTING?

I don't need to make my work more interesting, it is interesting enough.

WHAT IS THE MOST IMPORTANT THING ABOUT THE WORK YOU DO?

Most important is customer satisfaction, by producing the best quality work, offering the best service, and knowing that my clients are completely happy ensures that clients will return.

IS THERE A LOT OF PRESSURE IN YOUR CURRENT WORK/HOW DO YOU DEAL WITH THIS PRESSURE?

Working freelance carries a degree of pressure that I find stimulating and enjoy working with. The pressure is usually associated with emotional clients, mind changers and lack of time. In most cases this kind of pressure provides motivation and tends to bring out the best in me.

HOW DO YOU DEAL WITH MIND CHANGERS AND TIME RESTRICTIONS

When a client suddenly changes his or her mind at the last minute or when I have a big project to do and there is a tight schedule - I have to decide whether it's realistically possible to do this without the quality suffering. If I can't, I have to remain calm and try to deal with the situation in a manner that will ensure that I don't lose the client.

HOW DO YOU DEAL WITH EMOTIONAL CLIENTS

When dealing with emotional clients, I have to offer comfort and assurance whilst not getting too involved. I may feel like crying myself, but I have to bottle it all up until the end of the day.

WHAT ARE SOME OF THE PROBLEMS YOU ENCOUNTER IN YOUR WORK/CAN YOU THINK OF A PROBLEM YOU ENCOUNTERED IN YOUR CURRENT JOB AND THE STEPS YOU TOOK TO OVERCOME IT/ TELL US ABOUT SOME OBSTACLES YOU HAD TO OVERCOME IN THE PAST?

During the course of my freelancing experience, I have encountered various obstacles that I have had to overcome, such as supplies being delayed due to a postal strike, clients turning up late for appointments or forgetting to turn up all together.

To avoid the postal service issue re-occurring, I had to switch to a local supplier. Although the supplies were more expensive to purchase and I had to change to different brands of products, they didn't have to be delivered. I could pick the supplies up whenever demand required and the new brands, they turned out to be better than the brands I was using previously.

To ensure clients turn up, on time to their appointments, I began sending a reminder card to the client a few days before their appointment. Now, I very rarely encounter this issue.

HOW DO YOU KEEP ORGANISED/HOW DO YOU PLAN YOUR DAILY ACTIVITIES AND PRIORITIES/HOW DO YOU MANAGE YOUR TIME EFFECTIVELY?

I consider record keeping an important tool. I use a diary to record all issues and events, as well as the whiteboard, for issues that I have to be aware of constantly. I also use daily 'to do' lists, which helps me to organise and plan my time. A few levels of priority are assigned to various tasks and issues. Some of them may be important and urgent, urgent but not important, important but not urgent, and so on. Each priority reflects these criteria, importance and urgency - my experience in carrying out the tasks of my job helps me determine those priorities.

WHAT ACTION DO YOU TAKE WHEN YOUR PLANS AND SCHEDULES ARE UPSET BY UNFORESEEN CIRCUMSTANCES?

A good plan, be it daily, weekly, monthly, or a longer range one, should always leave some room for unforeseen circumstances, problems or developments that are difficult or impossible to predict. When I plan or schedule activities, I try to build in a degree of flexibility and adaptability, so the eventual changes and rearrangements can be done quickly and easily, with minimum delays or interruptions of any kind.

WHAT WAS THE MOST SERIOUS DISRUPTION TO YOUR USUAL WORKING PATTERN OR ENVIRONMENT/HOW DID YOU COPE/HOW DID THIS MAKE YOU FEEL?

I remember shortly after I began freelancing, there was a postal strike and my supplies were seriously delayed. I couldn't book many appointments until the stock arrived. I looked around but no local suppliers had the particular supplies that I needed. In the end I had to travel into London to pick up stock.

This experience made me realise that, although it was cheaper and more convenient to have the supplies delivered, it wasn't very reliable; which made me feel insecure, dependant on others and not in control.

To avoid this issue re-occurring, I switched to a local supplier. Although the supplies were more expensive to purchase and I had to change to different brands, they didn't have to be delivered. I could pick the supplies up whenever demand required and the new brands, they turned out to be better than the brands I was using previously.

WHAT IS DISCUSSED DURING THE CLIENT CONSULTATION/HOW LONG DOES IT LAST?

Every client has to undergo a thorough consultation which can last between 10 and 20 minutes, depending on whether it is a new or existing client and what the client wants. Effective communication between myself and the client is essential before beginning the hairdressing service, to ensure that the client's wishes are met.

This is the ideal opportunity for me to identify any factors that may limit or affect the service or products that I use, and also determine the most suitable technique and/or products used.

The client's requirements and expectations are discussed, with style books, photographs, fashion magazines, and wigs being used as aids to understanding proposed outcomes. At this stage, I check for any hair growth patterns that may adversely affect the required style and ascertain whether the client's hair type, texture, thickness and density suit the requested style.

The overall cost is then discussed and, if applicable, an appointment made.

WHAT FACTORS LIMIT OR AFFECT THE SERVICE?

The only factor that limits or affects the service include, the hair and/or scalp are unsuitable for the intended procedure, such as open sores, cuts and abrasions.

Work Experience General

TELL US ABOUT THE JOBS YOU HAVE HELD, INCLUDING RESPONSIBILITIES AND REASONS FOR LEAVING, AND BRING US UP TO PRESENT.

After leaving school, I originally trained and worked as a receptionist at Any Hair Salon. As a receptionist, my day to day duties included attending to enquiries, phasing appointments, ensuring the comfort of the clients while they wait, calculating client bills and collecting payments, cashing up, providing a point of sale for retail goods and cleaning and sterilization duties.

I enjoyed being receptionist and jack of all trades but I was always on the lookout for something I could concentrate fully on. In 1997, I began studying for my NVQ in hairdressing and when a trainee position opened up in April 1998, I seized the opportunity to apply.

My day to day duties included cutting and styling hair, advising clients on styles and treatments, holding consultations and providing aftercare advice.

In August 2000, I was promoted to senior hair stylist. With this came greater responsibilities such as supervising and training work experience students in the hair extension process. I remained in that position for over 2 years and gained a multitude of leadership experience but, if my career was going to develop in the way that I wanted, it was important for me to gain wider experience. Working freelance offered new challenges and gave more opportunity to work the hours I chose, and that would give me the time to work on advancing my career in the airline industry. So in February 2003, I made the move into freelance.

WHY DID YOU CHOOSE THE HAIR DRESSING INDUSTRY?
I have always been interested in hair fashion and have strong creative skill and so the decision to enter this profession came as a natural progression from that early interest.

I regard this field as a challenging and an interesting one, with many demands and a lot of hard work, but also full of opportunities to develop both my customer care and communication skills.

OUT OF ALL THE POSITIONS YOU HAVE HELD (INCLUDING FREELANCE), WHICH POSITION WAS YOUR FAVOURITE/GAVE YOU THE MOST SATISFACTION?
It's hard to pick a single favourite position because there have been aspects of every position that I've enjoyed, each for different reasons.

However, my most satisfying job to date has been my current one because it offers me the opportunity to use all of my initiative and skill to solve problems and get things done, whilst at the same time providing similar tasks to that involved in my previous positions.

OUT OF ALL THE POSITIONS YOU HAVE HELD (INCLUDING FREELANCE), WHICH POSITION WOULD YOU SAY WAS THE MOST BORING?
I haven't found any of the work in my career boring. I've always been too busy to be bored! There has been something interesting, something that held my attention, about every position I've held, or I don't think I would have been doing the job in the first place.

OUT OF ALL THE JOBS/POSITIONS YOU HAVE HELD (INCLUDING FREELANCE), WHICH POSITION DID YOU LEAST ENJOY?

Each position had its different challenges, and required me to utilise my knowledge, skills and experience to meet those challenges. This made my working environment stimulating and provided opportunities to develop in many ways. So I cannot really say what position I least enjoyed as each working experience was valuable.

No matter how much the recruiters probe, don't give in.

WHAT WAS THE LEAST ENJOYABLE EXPERIENCE IN YOUR WORK EXPERIENCE/EMPLOYMENT?

I cannot recall one particular moment or situation in my work history that I can say was the least enjoyable, mainly because I've always approach my career with a positive and enthusiastic attitude. When unfavourable situations occur, I see them as challenges and opportunities to learn.

IF PROBED FURTHER

Dealing with friends and acquaintances trying to pressure me into a low price is not a great experience.

WHAT WAS THE MOST ENJOYABLE EXPERIENCE IN YOUR WORK EXPERIENCE/EMPLOYMENT?

My most enjoyable experiences are usually a result of satisfied customers. I get a sense of happiness in making people happy. That feeling of pride when you see the clients face glow with happiness when their hair has been transformed, it's very satisfying and makes me proud to see what I have done.

IF ASKED FOR AN EXAMPLE

I remember a client who came to me after wearing sewn in extensions for 3 years. The extensions had caused damage to her natural hair and spots of baldness. After carefully applying the new extensions, I sent her home with a concentrated protein spray, and after 2 weeks, her hair felt healthy again, and she had tons of new growth. Needless to say, she is VERY happy!!

DESCRIBE A TIME WHEN YOU THOUGHT YOU WERE DOING WELL/WHEN WERE YOU MOST HAPPY AT WORK?

I am happy with the way things are going now; I have achieved everything I have set myself and more, and hopefully I am looking forward to an exciting new career as cabin crew.

DESCRIBE A TIME WHEN YOU FELT THINGS WERE NOT GOING WELL?

I remember shortly after I began freelancing, there was a postal strike and my supplies were seriously delayed. I couldn't book many appointments until the stock arrived. I looked around but no local suppliers had the particular supplies that I needed. In the end I had to travel into London to pick up stock.

This experience made me realise that, although it was cheaper and more convenient to have the supplies delivered, it wasn't very reliable; which made me feel insecure, dependant on others and not in control. To avoid this issue re-occurring, I switched to a local supplier. Although the supplies were more expensive to purchase and I had to change to different brands of products, they didn't have to be delivered. I could pick the supplies up whenever demand required and the new brands, they turned out to be better than the brands I was using previously.

HOW MANY DAYS HAVE YOU HAD TO TAKE OFF DUE TO SICKNESS/WHAT IS YOUR ATTENDANCE RECORD LIKE?

I'm proud to say that my attendance record has always been very good. I'm in excellent health, I don't have any allergies and I rebound quickly. I have never had to cancel an appointment due to sickness and in the whole time I was working at Any Hair Salon, I only took 3 days off for an extremely heavy cold, but I am usually pretty resilient and, more often than not, I manage to arrange any medical appointments around my schedule.

DO YOU ARRIVE AT WORK ON TIME?

Yes, I am usually the first to arrive in the morning and I dislike being late for anything. If I have a problem being on time – due to traffic, car trouble etc, I always call and explain the situation.

WHAT DO YOU FEEL IS A SATISFACTORY ATTENDANCE RECORD?

I believe it is every employee's responsibility to show up, on time, every work day. Days lost through sickness are unproductive and expensive and should only be taken when absolutely necessary. I think you owe it to your colleagues as well as your manager to be punctual.

CAN WE CONTACT YOUR PREVIOUS EMPLOYER FOR REFERENCES/WHAT WOULD THEY SAY?

Yes, of course you can check my references. I'm confident that all my references will be favourable and will confirm what we've discussed here today.

WHAT HAVE YOU LEARNED FROM YOUR WORK EXPERIENCE?

There are three general things I have learned from past experience. First, if you are confused, ask – it's better to ask a dumb question than make a stupid mistake. Second, it's better to promise less and produce more than to make unrealistic forecasts. And finally, I have learned that what is good for the company is good for me.

WOULD YOU RECOMMEND HAIRDRESSING/FREELANCING TO OTHERS?

Certainly; depending on what they are hoping to achieve and their attributes. It's interesting work for people who are good with their hands, patient, and understanding and have a genuine interest in people. I would have to warn anyone considering entering it now that it is very competitive and hard to get into, so they would have to be resilient as well as enthusiastic.

My advice to anyone starting up would be to get lots of salon experience before you even think of going freelance, make a lot of effort to keep up to date with videos and magazines and attend training seminars and workshops when opportunities arise.

HAVE YOU DONE THE BEST WORK YOU ARE CAPABLE OF?

That's hard to say, because I'm always striving to do better, but in doing so I increase my skills and therefore always see room for improvement. I have had some great accomplishments in my career, such as my success at working freelance, but I believe the best is yet to come.

HOW DO YOU FEEL ABOUT YOUR CAREER PROGRESS TO DATE?

In looking back over my career I am very satisfied with my progress, I have achieved all that I have set myself and more. I have identified opportunities that would stretch and develop me and have been pleased with my achievements. I have gained a great deal in terms of knowledge and experience, and I am now seeking to maintain this momentum.

DO YOU HAVE ANY REGRETS?

I don't regret the course of my career, because I have worked for an interesting company, with extraordinary people. I have got to learn from their advice, to better myself and ultimately, I have succeeded in my chosen profession.

IF YOU COULD START YOUR CAREER OVER AGAIN, WHAT WOULD YOU DO DIFFERENTLY?

I am satisfied with the direction and progress my career has taken to date and would not do anything differently. I now look forward to progressing further.

WHEN HAVE YOU WORKED UNSOCIABLE HOURS/HOW DID YOU COPE?

Working Freelance can involve working unsociable hours, during the busy periods. During these peak times, it is quite common for me to be working through the day, right into the late evening, typically 12 - 13 hours.

Because these are predictable periods when I expect to be kept busy, they are easy to plan for and therefore cope with.

WHAT ARE THE LONGEST HOURS YOU HAVE EVER WORKED?

Last winter, during the Christmas/new year period, business increased, which meant I had to work more hours than usual. During this period, I found myself working up to 60 hours each week. I can say that this is the longest hours I have worked.

HOW DID YOU COPE?

I coped fine, I have a lot of energy and I anticipated this period would be busy, so was prepared in advance.

PROFESSIONAL KNOWLEDGE AND EXPERIENCE

WHAT HAS BEEN THE MOST SIGNIFICANT ACHIEVEMENT UP TO THIS POINT IN YOUR CAREER?

Although I believe my biggest accomplishments are still ahead of me, I feel my most significant accomplishment to date was rising from the receptionist and general hand to become a hairdresser. I think it demonstrates not only my growth but also the confidence my manger had in my ability. I've accomplished many things in my career since, but I still look back on that one event as the turning point and the accomplishment that made all the others possible.

IN YOUR CURRENT/PAST POSITION, WHAT PROBLEMS DID YOU COME ACROSS THAT CAME AS A SURPRISE TO YOU?

By planning ahead, I can anticipate any potential problems and be prepared to deal with them. I keep comparing my current situation against my plan and take necessary action to correct any deviation. This helps me expect and prepare for problems rather than be surprised by them.

IN YOUR CURRENT/PAST POSITION, WHAT PROBLEMS DID YOU IDENTIFY THAT HAD BEEN PREVIOUSLY OVERLOOKED?

While I was working as a receptionist at Any Hair Salon, I identified that many clients were waiting longer than necessary when they arrived for their appointments because hairdressers had to wait for the client to arrive before they could set up the right equipment.

I realised this was because the appointment system that was being used was inefficient. When appointments were made, the only details recorded in the diary were the clients name and contact details. So from then on, I began entering as much detail as possible about the treatment required; therefore the hairdressers were able to set up the equipment before the client arrived. This was the most sensible alternative to the way things were done previously, which resulted in a cut of waiting times. Sometimes, all that's needed is the application of common sense.

WHEN HAVE YOU EXPERIENCED A PRESSURED SITUATION/TELL US ABOUT A TIME WHEN YOU HAVE BEEN PRESSURED BY AN AWKWARD OR DIFFICULT PERSON/TELL US ABOUT A TIME WHEN YOU HAD TO BE ASSERTIVE/WHEN HAVE YOU HAD TO SAY NO TO A CLIENT.

Example 1

I remember when an acquaintance of mine tried to pressure me into an extremely low price on the basis of friendship. I stood my ground and offered a reasonable discount and eventually she agreed to the discount I was offering, but then began insisting that I offer her the service on credit. I remained assertive and explained that I do not offer a credit facility. Eventually she accepted my reasons for not offering credit but I could sense she was not happy.

HOW DID YOU COPE/HOW DID THIS MAKE YOU FEEL?

This happens occasionally, so I have learnt not to take what is being said to heart and be more assertive in my response. At the end of the day, if I give in to everyone I know, I will not be in business for very long.

Example 2

I remember a client who was having a full colour and restyle done. Upon my arrival to the client's premises at 5pm, the client explained that due to last minute plans, she would need for me to finish her hair by 6pm. I explained that this would not be possible as the quality would seriously suffer. I suggested that she either re-schedule the appointment of re-organise her plans for a later time. The client disagreed with both suggestions and so I explained that I would complete her hair as quickly as I possibly could.

The client kept me continually updated with the time and then at 6pm began panicking that she was going to be really late and was going to lose her reservation. I made some further suggestions that I thought would free up some time, such as doing her make-up whilst I done her hair and also offered to give her a lift to her destination.

I completed her hair by 6.25pm and had her at the restaurant by 6.37pm, only 7 minutes late. The client was very grateful for my efforts.

HOW DID THIS MAKE YOU FEEL?

Pressured but also more focused on the task.

WHAT DID YOU LEARN?

I learnt that I really need to emphasise during the consultation how long is needed to complete the work.

WHY DIDN'T THE CLIENT CATCH A TAXI?

By the time the client rang to book a taxi, it was too late and there was a long wait for one to become available.

TELL US ABOUT A DIFFICULT SITUATION WHEN YOU PULLED THE TEAM TOGETHER/DESCRIBE A SITUATION WHEN THE TEAM FELL APART. WHAT WAS YOUR ROLE IN THE OUTCOME?

I can't remember ever being in that situation, most of my colleagues at Any Hair Salon worked well together and had strong feelings of belonging to the team, however I did face something slightly similar that I could tell you about?

...I remember one situation where two of my colleagues really didn't hit it off with one another. They were constantly quarrelling and everyone had lost patience with them but no one wanted to get involved.

In the end I grasped the nettle and decided to assert myself. I was not their manager, so it was not a case of using authority. I did have to be as tactful as I could, and I began by diplomatically explaining that I acknowledged their personal dislike for each other, and then I drew upon the fact that they were both professionals and can therefore put aside their differences for the good of the salon.

I persuaded them to talk so that they could work out an effective strategy for working together. They had a pretty frank discussion and although I can't say they ended up the best of friends, they did gain more respect for one another's roles and certainly worked more productively together. I was really glad I had taken the initiative.

WHAT WAS THE MOST DIFFICULT SITUATION YOU HAVE FACED/HOW DID YOU COPE/HOW DID YOU FEEL?

I remember when I was 16, my younger brother, who was about 6 years old at the time, had a convulsion. I was alone with him at the time and at first I was a little scared, but I knew I had to do something, and moved quickly to ring the emergency services.

I remained calm and as directed, I put a pillow under his head, loosened his clothes around his neck and removed nearby objects that he may damage himself on. His tongue was floppy so was blocking the hole in his throat, which caused him to stop breathing. I was told not to put my finger in his mouth as he may bite it off; instead I was to roll him onto his side and wait for him to regain consciousness. I took several deep breaths and after a couple of minutes, he regained consciousness and the ambulance arrived.

This was the most worrying experience I have had to deal with, but I remained calm and managed to keep my emotions under control.

TELL US ABOUT A TIME WHEN YOU HAVE BEEN PRESSURED BY AN AWKWARD OR DIFFICULT PERSON?

It doesn't happen very often, but I do remember when an associate of mine tried to pressure me into an extremely low price on the basis of friendship. She tried using guilt tactics but I stood my ground and offered a reasonable discount and eventually the situation was solved.

It can be a big problem when making the transition from a hobby to business, but it is up to me to let everyone know I am a professional and ask for their support.

HOW DID YOU COPE/HOW DID THIS MAKE YOU FEEL?

This happens occasionally, so I have learned not to take what is being said to heart and to be more assertive in my response. If I don't stand my ground, I will not be in business for very long.

WHAT HAS BEEN THE BIGGEST DISAPPOINTMENT OF YOUR CAREER?

I couldn't say that I have had any big disappointments in my career. I've been doing the type of work I like and that makes good use of my knowledge and experience. However I was a little let down when I didn't get onto a part time hairdressing course after leaving school and yet I ended up enjoying myself and doing well anyway, and eventually I managed to get myself on the course.

Naturally, if I don't get this job, it will be my biggest disappointment; it is something I really want.

WHAT DID YOU LEARN FROM THE EXPERIENCE?

My disappointment over this course made me start applying early to the courses that interested me so that I could avoid a further disappointment. I have never come across this problem since.

DESCRIBE A TIME WHEN YOU'VE HAD TO DEAL WITH AN ANGRY OR UPSET CUSTOMER/HOW DID YOU RESOLVE THE SITUATION?

I had a client who was booked in for highlights, but after examining her hair, I noticed she had a dry blistery scalp. As the health of my clients is important to me, I was not prepared to carry out the treatment as it may worsen the problem. The client was understandably very upset.

I listened to what she had to say and then apologised for the inconvenience. When I had managed to calm her down, I was able to explain that I was not prepared to take the risk for her own protection and explained that I would be happy to return to carry out the procedure once her scalp had healed. Although the client felt very disappointed, she waited several days. During this time, her scalp had healed and I was able to return to carry out the service.

WHAT WAS WRONG WITH HER SCALP?

The client had had an adverse reaction to a product that she had used a few days prior.

HOW DID YOU APPROACH THE CONVERSAITON?

I was polite, sympathetic and professional.

HOW DID IT MAKE YOU FEEL?

Health and safety is an important issue and one I take seriously. So although I felt disappointed for the client, I did not feel bad because I done what I felt was right.

TELL US ABOUT A TIME WHEN YOU WERE CONFRONTED BY SOMEONE SHOUTING AT OR BEING ABUSIVE TOWARD YOU/HOW DID YOU COPE/HOW DID THIS MAKE YOU FEEL?

I have not been put in such a situation before mainly because I do not give people reasons to be that away inclined but, in being faced with this situation I would always take the person concerned into a private area where I can calm things down and talk to them in private.

HOW EXACTLY WOULD YOU DEAL WITH THEM?

If available, I would offer a cup or tea, and then I would listen to what they have to say.

I would let them get the whole thing off their chest and show that I am listening by; asking for clarification where appropriate, summarising, using the appropriate body language, and making notes where appropriate.

I would then investigate the facts because, whatever I feel personally about the situation, I cannot deny their feelings of anger or disappointment and whether the person is justified or not, something has angered them, so whatever it was could anger someone else. I need to find out what has happened and, learn from it.

If at any point I feel uncomfortable or even in danger when someone is shouting or showing signs of becoming physically aggressive, I would simply walk away. I would explain my action and specify the consequences of certain behaviour. If I judge it to be necessary, I would not hesitate to ask for help.

WHAT HAS BEEN YOUR GREATEST PROFESSIONAL MISTAKE/WHAT WAS THE BIGGEST MISTAKE YOU HAVE EVER MADE?

The biggest mistake was providing my service to a friend on credit. Not only was it extremely difficult to retrieve the money, but once the message got around, everybody else began expecting the same treatment.

Unfortunately, it really was my fault. I learned from the experience and I have never made the same mistake since.

HOW HAVE YOU BENEFITED/LEARNED FROM YOUR DISAPPOINTMENTS?

I have learned a lot from disappointments, either my own or those of others. I wouldn't call them disappointments as such, just temporary setbacks. Whenever I encounter disappointment, my first task is to look at what happened, why it happened, and how I would do things differently in each stage should the same set of circumstances appear again. That way I never repeat mistakes and always anticipate potential problems.

Or

I treat every disappointment as a learning experience. Whenever I have a disappointment, my first task is to analyse what went wrong and how it could have been prevented. That way, I put disappointment behind me and am ready with renewed confidence and understanding to face the new day's problems.

HOW HAVE YOU BENEFITED/LEARNED FROM YOUR MISTAKES?

I have learned a lot from mistakes, either my own or those of others. Whenever I make a mistake, I acknowledge the error, and use it as a lesson to keep me from making the same mistake again. That way I never repeat mistakes and always anticipate potential problems. We all make mistakes; it's what we do with the lessons learned from our mistakes that determine our success in life.

For example... The mistake I made in providing my service to a friend on credit made me think twice before giving anyone credit in the future, I have never made the same mistake since.

HOW DO YOU PREPARE YOURSELF FOR POTENTIAL PROBLEMS?

I prepare for potential problems by analysing past problems In any case, I think of problems as opportunities to be creative.

WHAT DO YOU DO WHEN YOU HAVE TROUBLE SOLVING A PROBLEM?

One thing I don't do is ignore it and hope it will go away. I stand back and examine the problem. I make a list of possible solutions, weighing both the consequences and cost of each solution to determine the best course of action. I then present my planned solution to those who will be affected by it and seek advice and/or approval.

HOW DO YOU HANDLE FAILURE?

Naturally failing hurts my feelings however, I am not one to give up quickly. I treat every failing as a learning experience; I look at what went wrong, why it went wrong, and how I would do things differently should the same set of circumstances appear again. That way, I put failure behind me and am ready with renewed confidence and understanding.

WHAT HAS BEEN THE BIGGEST FRUSTRATIONS IN YOUR CAREER?

I've always approached my career with enthusiasm, so I really haven't experienced much frustration. When I do find myself up against a source of frustration, I convert it into an opportunity to prove myself and set an example for others to follow.

HOW DO YOU APPROACH DIFFICULT SITUATIONS?

I approach difficult situations in a calm and objective way and am polite yet resolute when handling a difficult customer. I try to seek acceptable outcomes and am undaunted if solutions cannot always be found.

HOW OFTEN HAVE YOU MISSED DEADLINES AND WHAT WERE THE OUTCOMES?

I rarely miss deadlines, owing to my planning and organising skills and general project management abilities. My experience plays an important role in anticipating the problems and prevention of the things that could go wrong. Good planning and effective control over the work is the most effective weapon in the battle with time and mounting costs.

GIVE ME AN EXAMPLE OF A PROBLEM YOU ENCOUNTERED THAT DIDN'T WORK OUT

My bank returned my client's cheque to me through lack of funds. I was sure this was a mistake caused through an oversight on the part of my client. I tried ringing the client on several occasions so that I could explain the situation and agree a time when I would collect the money. Failing that, I went round to the client's house. I left a note but never heard back. At this point, I had to decide whether to write off the debt and blacklist the client or visit the Citizens' Advice Bureau for advice on retrieving the funds. After careful consideration of all the factors involved, I decided to write the debt off. I learned from the experience and I now wait for the funds to clear before carrying out a service.

TELL US ABOUT A TIME WHEN YOU SOLVED A CUSTOMER PROBLEM

I solve customer problems all the time, however, I remember one problem in particular. I had a client who had previously worn sewn in extensions for 3 years, which had caused damage to the natural hair and spots of baldness. After carefully applying the new extensions, I sent her home with a concentrated protein spray, and after 2 weeks, her hair felt healthy again, and she had tons of new growth. Needless to say, she is VERY happy!!

PLEASE BRIEFLY RELATE AN EXPERIENCE WHERE YOU WERE ESPECIALLY PLEASED WITH THE SERVICE/ASSISTANCE YOU WERE ABLE TO GIVE SOMEONE/WHEN HAVE YOU GONE OUT OF YOUR WAY FOR A CLIENT?

Example 1

I remember a client was asking for a particular product that she had been recommended. The client had searched around for this product but hadn't had any luck in tracking it down. I knew I could get this product from the wholesalers where I collected my supplies from but it was not available for purchase by the general public, so I offered to help her by collecting the product for her. She was very happy and grateful for my efforts, which gave me a sense of self satisfaction.

Example 2

When I first went freelance, the process of my work was to provide the service within the client's home or chosen premises. I encountered a problem when one of my clients was unable to have the service carried out in her home because it was in the process of being redecorated. I rang a contact I had within a local salon and was able to arrange to carry out the service within the salon for a small fee. This worked out really well because the salon was in a location that was convenient for both myself and the client to travel to.

HOW DO YOU DEAL WITH A DIFFICULT CUSTOMER?

Example 1

I remember when I had a consultation with a client and we agreed on the colour and style she wanted to have done. When her appointment date came round, she had decided to go for something completely different. As a result, I had to reschedule her appointment in order to purchase different products. At times like this, I have to be patient, calm, professional and understanding.

HOW DO YOU PREVENT THIS SITUATION RE-OCCURING?

I have to really emphasise during the consultation how important it is that the client keeps me informed of any changes.

Example 2

I recall a time when I had carried out a cut and highlights on a client, it had taken me about 2 and a half hours to complete and I was satisfied with the final result and thought it was one of the best I had done. This however was not consistent with the clients feelings as she didn't feel it suited her and wasn't happy with the final result. After some deliberation, she insisted on having her hair put back t its original colour. She apologised for having wasted my efforts but agreed to pay me for my time. She later rescheduled an appointment for a different colour and was satisfied with the final result.

HOW DID THIS MAKE YOU FEEL?

At first I was disappointed, but this made me realise that what I like is not necessarily what someone else will like. My main concern is that I leave the client happy and content.

DID YOU TRY TO PERSUADE HER TO KEEP THE HIGHLIGHTS?

Yes, I explained that it was probably just the initial shock and therefore she should give herself a few days to see if she gets used to the colour and if she still didn't like it after this time, I would happily return to remove the colour.

HOW DO YOU PREVENT THIS SITUATION RE-OCCURING?

I have to really emphasise during the consultation that the results of a different colour, whether it be partial highlights or full head of colour, will create a dramatic result and so are they absolutely sure they want to go ahead. I also began using wigs and hairpieces to give an example of what the final result will look like, that way, I am sure they are completely happy to go ahead.

WHEN HAVE YOU HANDLED A CUSTOMER COMPLAINT?

I remember when I was working on reception at Any Hair Salon and a client rang to complain about a perm that she had had done. I knew the customer wasn't happy, so I gave her chance to talk while I listened. This seemed to calm her down. Once she had finished what she wanted to say, I told her that I could understand her disappointment and apologised for the situation.

I immediately offered her an appointment so that the stylist could examine her hair and identify the cause of the problem and if necessary re-perm the dropped side. The client said that would be fine. I thanked her for her understanding and immediately booked her an appointment.

The client later told me that I was very caring and professional and she later sent a complimentary letter about me to the salon manager. It made me feel good that I was able to turn her experience into a positive one and as a direct result, the client became a regular visitor to the salon.

WHY HAD THE PERM DROPPED?

The client's hair was fairly fine and one side had simply taken better than the other.

TELL US ABOUT THE BIGGEST CHALLENGE YOU HAVE FACED/HOW DID YOU RESPOND TO THAT CHALLENGE?

To be honest – giving up smoking was the biggest challenge. I never thought I could do it and I had had dozens of attempts that ended in failure. It isn't just the fact that I don't smoke any more. I have gained so much personal insight and I deal with potentially stressful situations at work so much more effectively now, I feel more energetic, more mentally alert and far calmer now than I ever did before.

HAVE YOU EVER MISINTERPRETED ANY INSTRUCTIONS, MESSAGE OR INFORMATION/WHAT WAS THE OUTCOME OF THOSE SITUATIONS?

No, I am pleased to say that I haven't. I always devote my exclusive attention to the person speaking to me. That way most misunderstandings can be eliminated and effective communication established. I notice that most poor listeners, when they are not talking, are busy rehearsing what they are going to say next. That way it is very difficult to exchange ideas and messages.

SKILLS & ABILITIES

Personal Traits & Skills

Communication/Interpersonal Skills

Decision Making

PERSONAL TRAITS AND SKILLS

My Views

WHAT ARE YOUR BEST QUALITIES/GREATEST STRENGTHS?

I have very good interpersonal skills and I pride myself on being able to build rapport quickly with new people. To me, establishing rapport seems to be a natural tendency. In fact, at Any Hair Salon, I was often asked to carry out the shampoo because the manager knew I would make the clients feel welcome and important.

I am always professional and adopt a mature approach to my work. I keep calm and don't let attention to detail slip when there is a lot of pressure and can be relied on to pull with the team when it's facing any kind of challenge.

I'm driven to achieve, to surpass my most recent record, so you'll never see me deliver merely acceptable performance and communicate well with my superiors and colleagues at all times,

I feel that for the above reasons I would be successful as cabin crew and would be a valuable asset to XXX Airlines.

WHAT QUALITIES ARE YOU NOT SO PROUD OF/ WHAT IS YOUR GREATEST WEAKNESS?

I can, on occasion, be a bit of a perfectionist. I tend to spend longer than necessary making sure that things are perfect and sometimes get a little frustrated if I don't achieve excellence. I did learn early on in my career that this slows output, but on the other hand, without such attention to detail, the consistency and accuracy of my work could be affected. It is a difficult balancing act but I am working on finding a more balanced approach, for example being contempt with satisfactory standards.

IN WHAT WAY ARE YOU A PERFECTIONIST?

I set myself high standards, which means I am not satisfied until I have surpassed satisfactory standards.

WHAT ARE YOUR 3 GREATEST STRENGTHS AND WEAKNESSES?

Strengths

Delivering customer care

Communication skills

Managing adversity

Weaknesses

I expect high standards

I sometimes work too hard

It's hard to think of anything which comes to mind, however if I had to choose a third weakness, it would be chocolate.

HOW HAVE YOU CHANGED IN THE LAST 5 YEARS?

I feel like I have matured-rather than aged 5 years. The skills I have acquired and the qualities I have developed have changed me enormously and I know there are parts of me that are not being utilised half as effectively as they could be.

Each position I have carried out has given me an opportunity to develop my communication, interpersonal and problem solving skills, I have learnt how to work successfully with others, how to deal effectively with suppliers and clients and how to motivate and be motivated. I have also greatly enhanced my people management and leadership skills. All of these will benefit my performance as a cabin crew member.

DO YOU CONSIDER YOURSELF A FUTURE, PRESENT, OR PAST ORIENTATED PERSON?

I try to live in the present, thinking in terms of what needs to be done now, instead of thinking about the past or worrying about the future. The past experiences are always valuable, and making plans for the future is an important business activity, but I endeavour to concentrate my efforts on current problems and issues.

WOULD YOU CLASSIFY YOURSELF AS A HARD-WORKING OR RELATIVELY LAID BACK?

When it comes to my job, I don't have time to be laid back. When I'm at work, I always give my best and try to achieve as much as possible. Of course, it is necessary to slow down from time to time to analyse my performance and plan future activities. Then, the hard driving starts again. I have always been self-motivated and not to work hard would be against my personal beliefs.

ARE YOU AN INTROVERT OR EXTROVERT?

I am quite extrovert, but I'm not so dependant upon other people that I get withdrawal symptoms when left alone.

or

I enjoy company, but can easily spend time alone and enjoy that too. I am by no means cautious but I feel no compulsion to take risks or to involve myself in situations where the spotlight is on me.

DO YOU HAVE AN ANALYTICAL MIND?

In the sense that I can identify problems and work out solutions to them, yes. I have above average analytical skills. Like everything else, good analytical skills come through practice, through using that amazing computer between your ears on a regular basis. That's why I'm looking for work that requires me to think and act.

RATE YOURSELF ON A SCALE FROM 1 TO 10

I would rate myself as an 8. I always give my best, but in doing so I increase my skills and therefore always see room for improvement.

DO YOU CONSIDER YOURSELF A SMART PERSON?

Yes. That means I'm smart enough to know my opinion is biased. The kind of intelligence required on the job isn't always measured by IQ. Only through coping with different situations and interacting with other people can intelligence truly be judged. By these criteria, I'm above average in intelligence.

When it comes to working with people, solving business problems, and making decisions – especially those related to the job – I'm as good as or better than anyone else. There are many things I don't know, but I can learn. In that way, a smart person is one who asks questions, listens carefully, and realises nobody knows everything.

Or

To me, smart people are not necessarily the ones with high IQs. Education and intelligence is the ability to meet life's situations and perform in the job to the best of one's abilities. We show our value by the way we deal with people, approach business problems and make decisions.

With that in mind and without any false modesty I would consider myself a smart person. Of course, there are many things I don't know, but I make constant learning and self-improvement my main goal. To me, to be smart means to ask questions, listen to what people say, apply knowledge and know-how to problems and learn from my own and, preferably, from other people's mistakes.

DO YOU CONSIDER YOURSELF ASSERTIVE OR AGGRESSIVE?

I think the word I would use to describe myself would be assertive, rather than aggressive. When I think of an aggressive person, I think of someone who bullies or steamrolls others to get his or her way. Being assertive, on the other hand, allows me to make my ideas known without disparaging the ideas and opinions of others. It allows for a mutually fulfilling, two way exchange, without anyone being put down or attacked.

Or

I would consider myself to be assertive rather than aggressive. I am not afraid to be honest and direct, even if I think that the response is not going to be popular. However, directness doesn't mean rudeness or an absence of tact. I accept my own good and bad characteristics and do not feel the need to put others down, or to win. I acknowledge my own needs and opinions directly and openly, risking rejection or refusal. My self esteem doesn't depend on the approval of others, but I can respond sincerely to them.

TELL US ABOUT A TIME WHEN YOU HAVE HAD TO BE ASSERTIVE?

I have to be assertive with friends and associates of mine who try to pressure me into low prices. Being assertive in this situation is especially challenging because I know the individual concerned.

WHAT DO YOU DO WHEN YOU FIND IT DIFFICULT TO DO YOUR BEST WORK?

I rarely find it difficult to do my best work, I am always motivated to give my best efforts, and there are always opportunities to contribute when you stay alert. When for various reasons, it becomes difficult to do my best work, I find myself driving to produce, to maintain my record of success.

WHEN DO YOU TEND TO DO YOUR BEST WORK, IN THE MORNING OR IN THE AFTERNOON?

The time of day usually has no impact on my efficiency and energy level, but I prefer morning hours for major tasks, and late afternoon or early evening for planning, design and catching up on paperwork. I rarely get tired, even when I work overtime – it's just that some periods during the day are better suited for particular activities.

WHAT MOTIVATES YOU TO WORK HARD?

I have always been self motivated. I like that winning feeling when I do a good job and the sense of achievement and job satisfaction motivate me to make even bigger efforts. I also like being surrounded by bright people who are capable, hard working and good team players; the energy and creativity people can activate in each other is amazing.

Other great motivators include: Daily challenges, personal growth, accepting responsibility, looking forward to achieving goals, encouragement to use creativity and initiative in finding new ways to do things and finally, respect for a job well done.

NAME 5 THINGS THAT MOTIVATE YOU

Tangible results

The opportunity to work as part of a talented team of individuals

Daily challenges

Personal growth

Encouragement to use creativity and initiative in finding new ways to do things

SO MONEY DOESN'T MOTIVATE YOU?

Although I consider remuneration an important motivational factor, it is a secondary importance. The job itself, its tasks, the work environment and the opportunity to learn and participate in new and exciting developments, and become an efficient member of the team, are to me the most significant aspects of a job.

ARE YOU A SELF STARTER?

Yes I am. I rarely need others to motivate me, as I am very directed by my own career and am the sort of person who enjoys taking the initiative. I can set expectations for my work that are usually higher than others set for me, and I can achieve them. I'm a quick study and can be up and running with a minimum of instruction and training.

Or

Yes, I do consider myself a self starter. I never rely on someone else's initiative, I take the initiative myself. As a self starter, I can identify problems, devise a plan of action and assume full responsibility for my activities and the successful completion of required tasks.

HOW DO YOU FEEL ABOUT ROUTINE TASKS AND IRREGULAR HOURS?

I accept that every role carries with it a certain amount of routine in order to get the job done. If my job involves repetitive work, it is my responsibility to carry it out to the best of my abilities. As for irregular hours I would expect to have an indication of my core hours but will work the hours that are necessary in order to fulfill the requirements of the role.

CHANGE DRIVES THIS ORGANISATION, HOW FLEXIBLE ARE YOU/HOW DO YOU DEAL WITH CHANGE?

I positively thrive on change. I like to know that each day is going to be very different, with its own set of decisions to make and problems to solve.

WHEN HAVE YOU HAD TO FACE MAJOR CHANGES IN YOUR PERSONAL LIFE OR WORK?

The biggest change I have faced was going freelance. Being responsible for organising my own time, finding my own clients and dealing with my own accounts is very different from working in a salon. Being freelance also means no colleagues, which was the biggest and hardest change. However, I found the change very refreshing and a great challenge; as well as learning to be independent, I have learned, responsibility, discipline, and hard work. Each of which will benefit my performance as a cabin crew member.

DO YOU GET BORED DOING THE SAME WORK OVER AND OVER AGAIN/DO YOU GET BORED WITH DETAIL?

No. Work is not necessarily entertaining; it is something that must be routinely and successfully accomplished time after time. That's why it is called work and why I am being paid to do it. Sometimes you just have to set your preferences aside and focus on what needs to be done – even if it isn't something new and exciting.

HOW OFTEN DO YOU LOOSE YOUR TEMPER?

I am patient, understanding, and easy to deal with and never lose my temper. I regard that sort of behaviour as counterproductive and inappropriate. By losing your temper, you cannot possibly resolve a problem – you can only make it worse. Even if you're completely right, losing your temper often destroys your ability to convince others that you are right. Maintaining an open and positive approach to problems and potential conflicts, helps to control temper.

WHAT ARE SOME OF THE THINGS THAT BOTHER YOU?

I enjoy my work and believe in giving value to my employer. Dealing with clock watchers and the ones who regularly get sick on Mondays and Friday's concerns me, but it's not something that gets me angry or anything like that.

HOW DO YOU DEAL WITH THESE TYPE OF PEOPLE?

I talk to them to find out if there is any resolve to problems which they may be encountering.

WHAT MAKES YOU ANGRY/TELL US ABOUT THE LAST TIME YOU FELT ANGRY/WHAT MAKES YOU IMPATIENT/TELL US ABOUT THE LAST TIME YOU FELT IMPATIENT.

Not much makes me angry or impatient, however I understand that situations can occur occasionally, but instead of getting angry or impatient, I exert my energy into maintaining my professional approach and conduct.

Or

That's an interesting question, because I am, generally speaking, a tolerant person and I bear troubles calmly. Instead of getting angry or impatient, I use the opportunity to look at my own attitude and take responsibility for my own thoughts, so I begin to focus on the positives, on how I am really feeling beneath all that anger. The results are quite dramatic, my whole demeanour changes very rapidly, I become aware that I am in control. Now I know that in any given set of circumstances, I have the freedom to choose my attitude and control my own thoughts.

CAN YOU TAKE INSTRUCTIONS AND NOT FEEL UPSET OR HURT?

Yes, I take instructions well and I recognise that it comes in two varieties, depending on the circumstances. There is carefully explained instructions then there are those times when, as a result of deadlines and other pressures the instruction might be brief and to the point. While I have seen some people get upset with that, personally I've always understood that there are probably other considerations I am not aware of. So I listen very carefully to directions and always keep my superior informed of my actions.

HOW DO YOU REACT TO CONSTRUCTIVE CRITICISM?

Criticism is vital to my continued growth, and I welcome constructive criticism that helps me operate better or produce better results. However, it is important for me to understand where my critic is coming from so that I know how to apply the feedback.

DESCRIBE A SITUATION WHEN YOUR WORK OR IDEA WAS CRITICISED

Example 1

I remember when I was working at Any Hair Salon and I suggested to my manager that the salon would benefit from offering a nail service as an addition to the current services that were currently offered as it would increase clientele and revenue.

My manager was not enthusiastic and dismissed the idea as she said it would incur a lot of extra overheads for the salon and also, she didn't want the extra responsibility of adding a new service.

After this discussion, I went away and done some research into the costs involved, I visited salons and suppliers for price lists and spoke to clients about what they thought of the idea and would they be inclined to use the service. I received some very positive feedback from this research and so decided to re-approach my manager with the information.

She spent some time looking over the information and done some research herself and also came back with positive results and subsequently agreed with the idea. A couple of months later, the service was added and a nail technician was hired. The result was, as expected, a dramatic increase in new clientele and revenue.

WHY DIDN'T YOUR MANAGER THINK OF THIS IDEA?
She thought there would be a lot of extra costs and responsibilities involved, she later realised that the costs were not very high and neither were the responsibilities.

HOW DID SHE INITIALLY RESPOND TO YOUR IDEA?
She explained that she was happy to see that I was enthusiastic about making the salon better but it was not something she was going to consider at that time.

HOW DID YOU RESPOND TO THE CRITICISM?
I thanked her for her time and explained that as I thought it was a good idea worth considering, I thought I would mention it.

HOW DID IT MAKE YOU FEEL?
I did not take it to heart as I felt it was constructive criticism and I realise now that I should have gathered facts and figures before I approached her with my idea.

WHY DIDN'T YOU DO RESEARCH BEFORE APPROACHING HER WITH YOUR IDEA?
I realise now that that is what I should have done, this is what I learnt from the experience.

WHY DID YOU SUGGEST A NAIL SERVICE IN PARTICULAR?

I had noticed that a lot of our clients had nail extensions, this meant that we already had potential clients coming into the salon before even advertising the service.

Example 2

I remember when I was holding a consultation with a client and the client asked for my opinion on what hair colour I thought would suit her. I examined her eyes and skin tone and then suggested that I thought a warm mahogany colour would suit her as it would really emphasise the colour of her eyes and compliment her warm complexion. The colour was completely different to what she currently had and she didn't approve to say the least. I gave her a strand of extension hair in the colour I had recommended and suggested that she take it away with her and maybe she would grow to like it. A couple of weeks later, she booked into the salon for a colour change and was pleasantly surprised with the final result and subsequently apologised for her initial reaction and harsh criticism.

WHY DID SHE CHANGE HER MIND?

When she left the salon, she told her friends about my suggestion and they agreed, this made her reconsider and later agreed herself. Also, the strand of extension hair I gave her had a positive impact.

HOW DID SHE RESPOND INITIALLY TO YOUR SUGGESTION?

She gasped and said no way, she said it was a horrible colour and far too dark.

HOW DID IT MAKE YOU FEEL?

I did not take it to heart because I knew that my suggestion would be a bit of a shock and also, I knew that what I like is not necessarily what someone else will like.

HOW DO YOU DEAL WITH CRITICISM/HOW DO YOU REACT TO CRITICISM THAT IS UNWARRANTED?

I try to see criticism as useful feedback on what I've done. When someone lets me have it, either fairly or unfairly, constructively or unconstructively, I first consider who is making the charges. It is important for me that I know where the critic is coming from, so that I know how to apply the feedback.

I look for the good in what the other person is saying. I don't read between the lines, nor add meaning or implications where none were intended. When the other person has finished, I ask any questions that are needed and seek recommendations or ideas that will readily improve the situation.

I would express regret over the situation then thank the person for raising the issue. If I intend to act on what I've heard, I let the other person know.

HOW WOULD YOU REACT IF YOU WERE CRITICISED ABOUT YOUR CONTRIBUTION?

Of course no one is perfect and there is always room for improvement. I welcome the opportunity to improve my performance.

HOW DO YOU HANDLE PERSONAL CRITICISM?

As long as the criticism is fair and constructive, I try to listen to it and remain gracious. I thank them for their candid feedback, and modify my future behaviour accordingly.

AND WHAT DO YOU DO IF THE CRITICISM IS NOT FAIR OR CONSTRUCTIVE?

I don't pay much attention to unwarranted criticism. I remain gracious and thank them for their input and concern.

HOW DO YOU MANAGE STRESS?

I always take time at the end of the day to reflect upon the days events and to analyse what I could have done better. When I notice prolonged problems, I take action to bring about change. I have found that taking time to reflect is a key element to managing stress.

Furthermore, I practise stress management through relaxation, rest and regular exercise and I avoid substances that can negatively affect my good health, such as cigarettes, alcohol and fast food.

I regularly go swimming and perform yoga and relaxation techniques which really help me to unwind and get ready for another day at work.

WHAT ARE THE 3 MOST IMPORTANT SKILLS THAT YOU HAVE DEVELOPED IN YOUR CAREER SO FAR?

Number one is easy; I've significantly improved my communication and interpersonal skills - working with colleagues, dealing with suppliers and members of the public. Number two; I've developed my problem solving skills – anticipating as well as solving problems, and as for number three; I've greatly enhanced my people management and leadership skills.

Each of these will transfer well and benefit my performance as a cabin crew member.

WHAT DON'T YOU LIKE TO DO?

I don't particularly enjoy doing paperwork, which seems to slow down the action. However, I realise the importance of documentation, so I cooperatively fill out any forms. But I'm always looking for efficiencies in that area that will get me out in front of the customer where I belong.

When there's something disagreeable to be done, I try to get it out of the way first.

WHAT ARE SOME OF THE THINGS YOU FIND DIFFICULT TO DO?

I find it difficult to do nothing; I have to be doing something.

WHAT ARE YOUR LIKES?

I like challenges. I always set personal goals to try and push myself that bit further and to feel I've achieved something.

WHAT SORTS OF CHALLENGES DO YOU LIKE?

I enjoy challenges that require me to use my initiative and problem solving skills.

WHAT ARE YOUR DISLIKES?

I try to be honest and act with integrity. I dislike it when others lie, blame or don't show the same commitment to the task or the company as I do.

HOW DO YOU DEAL WITH THESE PEOPLE?

I deal with these people in a professional and assertive manner and address the issues that are creating problems and conflict. Hopefully, by bringing the issues to the surface, this can help resolve the matter.

EXPLAIN BRIEFLY YOUR ATTITUDE AND APPROACH TO SELLING PRODUCTS OR SERVICES. WHAT METHODS DO YOU USE AND WHY?

My whole approach to selling is based on the fact that whenever we want to get cooperation from people, persuade them to buy something or win an argument, we have to speak in the other person's terms.

Before I try selling a product or service, I learn all about the features and benefits. Then I learn about the customer, their company, the products/services they are currently using and their needs. I determine what advantages my product/service had over their current product/service – price, quality, comfort, durability, or design, what would appeals to them. Then I make an appointment to meet with the decision maker to discuss their needs further. I encourage them to give me their ideas, (that way they feel they are coming up with the ideas, creating the designs and making decisions) I listen carefully, and then I make them aware of needs they hadn't realised before.

HOW WOULD YOU SELL ME THAT CH~~A~~

Before I'd try selling the chair to you, I'd learn
and benefits. Then I would learn about you, your ~~c~~
you are currently using and your needs. I'd
advantages my chairs had over your current chairs – ~~.~~y,
comfort, durability, or design, what appeals to you. ~~1~~ . ~~1~~ would
determine if you were the decision maker to whom I should make my
presentation. If so, I'd make an appointment to meet with you and
discuss your needs. I would encourage you to give me your ideas, I
would listen carefully, and then I would make you aware of needs you
hadn't realised before.

WHAT DO YOU CONSIDER YOURSELF GOOD AT DOING?

I consider myself good at providing exceptional customer care and working
well under pressure.

HOW WOULD YOU DESCRIBE YOURSELF/WHAT SORT OF PERSON ARE YOU?

I am a friendly, approachable person who has a genuine interest in people.
I readily adapt to new people and work environments, and demonstrate an
understanding of how to blend my personality with those possessed by
other people. I am always professional and adopt a mature approach to
my work. I am a rational, sensible and calm individual and can maintain
my standards when under pressure. I work well on my own initiative as
well as a team player and I deliver consistently excellent customer service.

IS YOUR MOST MEMORABLE CHARACTERISTIC/ THAT MAKES YOU STAND OUT FROM THE CROWD?

My most memorable attribute is my ability to remain calm and level headed while under pressure. I am a very rational person and never let my emotions cloud my rational thought processes.

I can remain calm when people around me are getting agitated and I am often the person who gets called on when there is a problem. On many occasions throughout my career and personal life I have demonstrated this capability. For instance...

I remember when I was 16, my younger brother, who was about 6 years old at the time, had a convulsion. I remained calm and moved quickly to ring the emergency services. This was the most worrying experience I have had to deal with, but I remained calm and managed to keep my emotions under control.

HOW DO YOU REMAIN RATIONAL?

By remaining positive, using my common sense and initiative and keeping my emotions under control.

IF YOU HAD TO CHARACTERISE YOURSELF IN ONE SENTENCE, WHAT WOULD YOU SAY?

I am a professional, friendly, confident, diplomatic person who has good communication, customer care and teamwork skills. However, I don't feel to characterise myself in one sentence is enough.

DESCRIBE YOURSELF IN 3 WORDS.

Composed, personable and energetic.

However, I don't feel to characterise myself in 3 word(s) is enough.

DO YOU WORK WELL UNDER PRESSURE/CAN YOU WORK UNDER PRESSURE?

I positively thrive on pressure – it makes me alert and very motivated and can force the release of untapped reserves of energy and initiative. However, there are limits and I try to avoid pressure becoming too great by enhancing my skills for dealing with pressure, re-evaluating my reaction to those situations, events, people or tasks which appear threatening to me, and increasing my fitness to cope; as a result, I avoid pressure becoming problematic.

HOW DO YOU RE-EVALUATE YOUR REACTION TO THREATENING SITUATIONS?

Imagining negative images creates a negative attitude, so it is important to react positively by replacing these negative images with positive ones. How you react to pressure depends very much on how you perceive it.

HOW DOES FITNESS ENABLE YOU TO COPE?

A strong body means a strong mind and thus stamina is important both physically and mentally.

HOW WELL DO YOU LEAD PEOPLE?

I've experienced good results from the leadership side of my work. I can communicate company goals and motivate people to produce. I'm pleased that those I initially trained and supervised eventually moved on to positions of greater responsibilities.

WHAT WOULD YOU SAY IS YOUR LEADERSHIP STYLE?

I adopt a varied style of leadership dependent upon the situation. However, generally speaking, I believe I am the kind of leader that draws colleagues with me, rather than one who pushes them from behind. I suppose I would describe myself as a bit of a shaper, good with new ideas and quick to spot how to delegate effectively and take on appropriate work myself.

Other People's Views

HOW WOULD A FRIEND DESCRIBE YOU?

They would say I am easy to get on with, have a good sense of humour, am quite outgoing, and am generally cheerful. They would also say I am someone who keeps personal commitments, protects personal confidences, and makes the time to help people.

HOW WOULD AN ENEMY DESCRIBE YOUR CHARACTER?

I don't have enemies that I know of, but if I did have, I suppose they might say that I am tenacious, brave, and driven.

WHY TENACIOUS

I am certainly not a person to give in without a struggle, but on the other hand, I'm quite realistic about my limits.

WHY BRAVE

I am prepared to confront issues when there is a need, and I'm not too concerned, but I weigh the consequences and don't act irresponsibly.

WHY DRIVEN

I know how to push for what I want, but can back off when it is advisable to do so.

DO YOU HAVE A COMPETITIVE NATURE?

Yes, a competitive nature is necessary to be successful in a corporate environment, but competitiveness doesn't mean steamrolling others to get my way. I am always competing with myself, trying to break my own record – to do something better and faster than the last time.

WHAT WOULD COLLEAGUES SAY ABOUT YOU/WHAT DO OTHER PEOPLE THINK OF THE WAY YOU WORK/WHAT DO OTHERS THINK ARE YOUR BEST QUALITIES/STRENGTHS?

It's a bit difficult to predict their response to this question. Judging by the successful and professional relationship I had with my colleagues, I would expect to be portrayed as hard working, motivated, a good communicator and a person of high integrity and moral. I believe they would also tell you that I am easy to get on with and am usually cheerful.

The formal feedback from my superiors was always very positive and they will tell you that I am a committed and enthusiastic member of the team, and am good with customers, I work well on my own initiative as well as with the team, I keep calm and don't let attention to detail slip when there is a lot of pressure and can be relied on to pull with the team when facing any kind of challenge.

ARE YOU SURE THEY WOULD BE THAT POSITIVE – THERE MUST BE ASPECTS OF YOUR PERSONALITY THAT SOME OF THEM WOULD BE LESS ENTHUSIASTIC ABOUT?

I am sure that my colleagues would agree with what I have said as we had a successful and professional working relationship.

HOW WELL DID SUPERIORS RATE PERFORMANCE/ WHAT DID SUPERIORS THINK ARE STRENGTHS/ IN WHAT AREAS HAVE YOU RECEIVED COMPLIMENTS FROM SUPERIORS?

My superiors always rated my job performance well, formally and informally. In fact, I was always rated as being capable of accepting further responsibilities. I received particularly favourable evaluations in the areas of customer care and working well with co workers. I have also received high ratings in the area of initiative and enthusiasm, because I look at each situation as a potentially exciting challenge, my superior's say I create excitement in other team members, which results in a greater team effort and higher output.

WHAT DID SUPERIORS THINK ARE YOUR WEAKNESSES?

What might be perceived by some as weaknesses are really my strengths, for example, I occasionally received comments about working too hard and putting in too many hours. They said that they thought I might be over-exerting myself and may burn myself out.

I see it as dedication and enthusiasm for my career and I personally don't feel I over-exert myself. Outside of work, I take time to relax and regularly go swimming, and practice yoga routines. This gives me a break from the work environment and keeps me stimulated.

RPERSONAL SKILLS

,HOWN GOOD COMMUNICATION/ ،LS?

deal with people on a daily basis, so being able to ıs a necessary part of my job.

My styı ، communication should establish a professional and caring relationship with the client. While the exact style that I use differs according to each individual, I must be courteous, friendly and professional, no matter who the client is or what my personal feelings are and I must not air my stresses or personal grievances with or in front of the client.

I recognise that these are key skills for a professional and successful business relationship.

HOW IMPORTANT IS COMMUNICATION WHEN DEALING WITH YOUR CLIENTS?

Unless you are aware of your client's wishes you will not be able to work towards satisfying them. Communication is the key.

or

Effective communication between me and the client is essential. Failure to communicate effectively with the client may result in failure to fulfil the client's wishes and loss of business.

WHAT ACTION DO YOU TAKE IF THERE ARE MEMBERS OF YOUR TEAM WHO REALLY DON'T GET ON WITH ONE ANOTHER, TO THE POINT WHERE THIS IS AFFECTING OTHER STAFF AND PERFORMANCE?

Most of my colleagues at Any Hair Salon worked well together and had strong feelings of belonging to the team. However, I do remember one situation where two of my colleagues really didn't hit it off with one another. They were constantly quarrelling and everyone had lost patience with them but no one wanted to get involved.

In the end I grasped the nettle and decided to assert myself. I was not their manager, so it was not a case of using authority. I did have to be as tactful as I could, and I began by diplomatically explaining that I acknowledged their personal dislike for each other, and then I drew upon the fact that they were both professionals and can therefore put aside their differences for the good of the salon. I persuaded them to talk so that they could work out an effective strategy for working together. They had a pretty frank discussion and although I can't say they ended up the best of friends, they did gain more respect for one another's roles and certainly worked more productively together. I was really glad I had taken the initiative.

WHAT WOULD YOU DO IF NO AMOUNT OF EFFORT ON YOUR PART SOLVED THE PROBLEM?

If after talking to them nothing changes or the situation worsens, I would need to consider seeking advice from a senior member of staff.

WHAT WAS THE TOUGHEST COMMUNICATION PROBLEM YOU HAVE FACED?

When I was visiting Gambia, I became acquainted with a French speaking lady. She understood my French, the little amount I knew, but she didn't really understand English. Unfortunately, the amount of French I knew wasn't enough to get me through a whole conversation, so I had to improvise.

To ensure she could understand, I used French wherever possible, was careful to avoid slang, jargon, acronyms, buzzwords, clichés, and colloquialisms and made more use of facial expressions and hand gestures. At first, it was a little tricky trying to find imaginative ways to communicate, but as time went on, it became much easier. Now when I encounter this type of communication barrier, I am much more confident in my ability to cope.

TELL US ABOUT A TIME THAT YOU HAD TO BE TACTFUL

I have to be tactful all the time in my work. Clients tell hairdressers all sorts of very personal things, particularly when they are in their own home and they know the information is confidential. This means I have to be discreet with personal issues, sensitive to problems and diplomatic in my response, whilst not getting too involved.

HOW CONFIDENT ARE YOU ABOUT ADDRESSING A GROUP?

I used to be nervous about speaking in front of a group, yet I found that preparation, practice and knowing my subject helped me overcome this, I now have no problem addressing a group.

HOW DO YOU HANDLE CONFLICT/IF YOU HAVE A DISAGREEMENT WITH A COLLEAGUE, HOW DO YOU HANDLE IT?

Collaborating is a problem solving approach, based on the principle that conflict can be managed so that nobody loses completely. I try to use this approach when dealing with conflict, because it does not focus on right or wrong, or who is to blame, but sees defining the problem and seeking a solution as a joint activity. Sometimes solutions emerge that neither side would have come up with independently. It is both analytical and flexible. You listen to others points of view and work to find a solution that is as good as it can be.

Collaborating in problem solving is the most productive way to handle conflict. The approach works towards a win-win situation, in which all those involved feel as if they have gained something in the process.

TO HANDLE A CONFLICT SITUATION

* Acknowledge the conflict exists
* Tackle conflict early to avoid it escalating
* Plan how to deal with the conflict
* Think it through
* Don't handle conflict in public/Set the scene/Identify common ground
* Raise the issue/Open it up/Talk it through/Get more information/Agree on what the problem is
* Refrain from offering my own opinion before understanding the full picture
* Try to avoid instinctive reactions
* Stay assertive
* Don't take it personally (unless it is personal)

- Don't fight anger with anger
- Pay attention to verbal and non-verbal communication
- Generate ideas
- Find solutions
- Agree on further action

Not all conflict at work is necessarily bad. People sometimes believe that conflict means there is a breakdown in communications or that one party simply doesn't get it. Even fully functional, rational people can view situations differently. Thus conflict may help bring different views and opinions to the surface so that ultimately a team can achieve great synergy and the desired results.

DECISION MAKING

AFTER YOU'VE MADE A DECISION, DO YOU STICK WITH IT?

Generally, yes, because I have found that my problem-solving and decision making methods work. But I am flexible, and when a proposed solution clearly isn't getting the expected results, I modify. Sometimes a minor change will make a major difference.

DO YOU CONSIDER YOURSELF TO BE THOUGHTFUL AND ANALYTICAL OR DO YOU USUALLY MAKE UP YOUR MIND FAST?

I would consider myself a little bit of both, I put thought and planning into any decision I make while having an awareness of the timescales involved.

WHAT DECISIONS DO YOU DISLIKE MAKING?

The kinds of decisions I dislike making, are the ones which result in customer dissatisfaction, such as having to cancel or postpone an appointment for example. When the client is dissatisfied, I feel dissatisfied. However, I accept that these kinds of decisions cannot always be avoided, and so I deal with them efficiently as they arise and try to arrive at a solution that produces the best results for the company while minimising the effects on the customer.

HOW DO YOU GO ABOUT MAKING IMPORTANT DECISIONS?

Before I act, I think. I evaluate my options and examine them objectively, weighing up possible outcomes, pros and cons, etc. I then rely on past experiences, company policies, intuition and common sense to guide me to a decision. I present my planned solution to those who will be affected by it - the staff, as well as those who will be called upon to explain my decision - my superiors. I then implement appropriate input and suggestions,

THE ULTIMATE CABIN CREW INTERVIEW Q&A BOOK

where necessary. I believe in immediate but realistic solutions to problems.

Or

Before making an important decision, I take three basic steps. First, I analyse all aspects of the issue and all possible consequences. Second, I try to anticipate potential problems that can affect the decision or be caused by it. Third, I talk to people who would be affected by that decision and get their input. By following these rules I make sure that the right decision is made.

WHAT DECISIONS DO YOU FIND MOST DIFFICULT?
It's not that I have difficulties making decisions – some just require more consideration than others.

WHAT WAS THE MOST DIFFICULT DECISION YOU HAVE MADE?
The decision to leave the comfort and security of my full time job to become freelance was definitely the hardest I have had to make. Making the right decision required a lot of fore thought and looking at best – and worst case scenarios extensively before making my decision.

I carried out independent research and already had a few clients to start off with, but still found the decision difficult because I knew that, at the end of the day, there are no guarantees that people will use the service.

Thankfully I went ahead and the outcome was positive.

GENERAL MOTIVES & PERCEPTIONS

Knowledge About & Suitability for the Job

Obviously, no one can tell you why you want the job, but it is crucial you consider this question both from your own, and the airline's perspective. If for example all you want is travel, and you cannot convince your recruiters that you would enjoy looking after their passengers, being a member of their cabin crew team, and being with their organisation, then you are probably ruling yourself out of contention!

When asked about your own personal qualities, it is sensible to emphasise those that are relevant to the role. Candidates who have not considered how the job will impact on their life will seem naive.

If you are asked about disadvantages, it would be best to choose the main drawbacks for your own circumstances, and then be prepared to say how you intend to overcome them!

Asking you to compare yourself with other candidates is unfair, but if this does come up you should stress your best qualities and why these would enable you to make a positive contribution to the airline's fortunes, rather than being negative about others.

KNOWLEDGE AND SUITABILITY FOR THE JOB

Cabin Crew

WHAT DO YOU THINK THE ROLE OF CABIN CREW INVOLVES/WHAT DO YOU THINK IS THE PRIMARY RESPONSIBILITY OF CABIN CREW?

Cabin crew are on board an aircraft for safety reasons. In the event of a real life emergency, the cabin crew must ensure that passengers follow the captains instructions, use safety equipment correctly and stay as calm as possible.

During the flight, the cabin crew spend a lot of time looking after the comfort of passengers. This involves giving special attention to children travelling alone, disabled people or people who are ill. Crew must appear friendly and sympathetic to anyone needing help, advice, reassurance, sympathy or even, at times, firm persuasion.

Other duties during the flight include preparing and serving meals and drinks and clearing up afterwards, selling duty free goods, and helping passengers to use in-flight entertainment systems. There is also paperwork to complete, this can include flight reports, customs and immigration documents, accounts of duty free sales and meal and drink orders.

At the end of the flight, the crew make sure the passengers leave the aircraft safely.

WHAT KIND OF INDIVIDUAL DO YOU THINK WE ARE LOOKING FOR TO FILL THIS ROLE?

I believe you are looking for an individual who has good communication, teamwork, and customer care skills and displays desirable traits such as maturity, friendliness, approachability and a sense of humour. The successful candidate would also need to have the ability to remain calm and level headed in emergency situations and be totally flexible about working with new people, flying different routes and working unsociable hours.

WHAT QUALITIES DO YOU HAVE THAT YOU FEEL WOULD MAKE YOU A GOOD CABIN CREW MEMBER?

My skills and experience closely matches the major requirements and diverse responsibilities for this role. Plus I will bring a depth of practical knowledge and experience that will transfer well and benefit my performance as a cabin crew member.

I am used to working under pressure and to tight time scales and I thrive on the challenges that these situations create.

Furthermore, I am an experienced team player and always work hard to support and contribute towards the overall team goal for success. I am a people person and would consistently deliver excellent customer service to passengers of all levels and I'm driven to achieve, to surpass my most recent record, so you'll never see me deliver merely acceptable performance.

I feel that both my personal qualities and the skills and experience I have gained from working in client-facing roles for the past 8 years would make an excellent member of Cabin Crew.

ARE YOU WILLING TO START AS A TRAINEE?

Yes, definitely. This is a new area for me, and I believe in getting a good foundation in the basics before progressing. An entry level position will enable me to learn the business inside out, and will give me the opportunity to grow when I prove myself. I also have a great deal of knowledge and work experience, which I'm sure, will contribute to my rapid progress through training. I am sure I shall learn quickly and I see it as a really exciting opportunity.

DO YOU KNOW ANYTHING ABOUT CABIN CREW TRAINING?

The training lasts for 5 weeks, and subjects covered include: Safety and emergency procedures, such as fire fighting, first aid, security and hijack procedures, and crowd control. Also covered is dealing with passengers and foreign currency and personal grooming and deportment. This initial period is followed by further on-the-job training, and usually a period of regular on board assessment.

HOW DO YOU FEEL ABOUT THE 6 MONTH PROBATIONARY PERIOD?

I can see no problem with a probationary period. I am a fast learner and it shouldn't take me long to prove myself.

WHAT QUALITIES DO YOU THINK A GOOD CABIN CREW MEMBER SHOULD HAVE/WHAT DO YOU THINK IT TAKES TO BE A SUCCESSFUL CABIN CREW MEMBER/HOW MANY OF THOSE QUALITIES DO YOU HAVE?

Passengers generally spend more time with the cabin crew than with any other members of the airlines staff, so they have a vital role in giving a good impression of the airline as a whole. This means cabin crew members need to have good communication and customer care skills and display desirable traits such as sincerity, a spirit of enthusiasm, confidence and a sense of humour.

They must be totally flexible about working with new people, flying different routes and working unsociable hours. They may deal with money, including foreign currency, so they should be honest as well as confident with numbers. Team working skills are also very important as is being fairly self contained, and satisfied in your own company.

The ability to manage change and adversity is another necessary quality for cabin crew. They should be able to show that they have strength of character to cope, which means approaching difficult and emergency situations in a calm and objective way – and being polite yet resolute in handling an abrasive customer.

These are all attributes that I possess and is the primary reason why I will make an excellent member of cabin crew.

DO YOU THINK THE ROLE OF CABIN CREW IS GLAMOROUS?

Well, it certainly is perceived as glamorous and it certainly has its benefits of travel. People see cabin crew in action, jetting around the world and form an immediate impression of what they think the job involves. In fact, the customer sees only a fraction of what goes on in order to make each flight a success. The truth is, cabin crew have to combine working as a flying waiter or waitress, mobile shop assistant, cleaner, plus all the emergency services rolled into one. It can be an exhausting and disorientating lifestyle that places tough demands on family and social commitments.

Therefore, no, I don't see the position of cabin crew as a glamorous role but rather a challenging role.

WHAT DO YOU THINK ARE THE DISADVANTAGES OF THIS POSITION/HOW WILL YOU COPE WITH THE DISADVANTAGES/ WHAT PROBLEMS DO YOU THINK YOU'LL FACE IN THIS JOB?

Having thoroughly researched this position, I expect that this job will present the usual risks that present other travellers, such as theft of personal belongings, bites and stings from insects, jet lag and service disruptions, to name but a few issues. However, I have considered these issues before I applied and will be sure to take any preventative measures necessary, such as carrying travellers cheques or bank card rather than lots of cash, using an insecticide or other similar product and in the case of jet lag, control food and water intake before the flight and get plenty of sleep.

So by being aware of these issues, they appear to be minor issues rather than disadvantages.

EXTRAS TO REMEMBER

Some would think that working different shifts would be a disadvantage; however, I enjoy a variable schedule.

I relish a challenge and there's nothing that I've seen in this job that intimidates me in any way.

WHAT DO YOU THINK ARE THE ADVANTAGES OF THE POSITION?

Working as a Cabin Crew member is not just a job, but a way of life and provides an alternative and very stimulating lifestyle where no two working days are likely to be the same. The sheer dynamics of different crew, passenger profiles, destinations and roster structures ensure that there will always be variety.

Furthermore, there are opportunities to visit places and experience cultures that are beyond most peoples reach. Cabin crew go to places they always dreamed of and find interest in destinations they would not necessarily have chosen to go to.

Additionally, it is a good feeling to deliver businessmen to their meetings on time, reunite family and friends; deliver newly weds to their honeymoon destinations, or vacationers to their dream holiday place. There is genuine feeling of doing something worthwhile, in a unique way which not many jobs regularly produce at the end of a hard day.

WILL YOU BE ABLE TO COPE WITH THE CHANGE IN ENVIRONMENT?

Definitely; I welcome the challenge of learning about and adapting to a new environment, that's one of the reasons I'm seeking to make a career change right now. Any major change, while always containing some challenge, is a chance to grow, learn, and advance.

WHAT DO YOU EXPECT FROM THIS JOB?

I expect that the role will provide an alternative and very stimulating lifestyle where no two working days are the same. The sheer dynamics of different crew, passenger profiles, destinations and roster structures ensure that there will always be variety. It's a job I will find very rewarding in a number of ways.

WHAT WILL YOU LOOK FORWARD TO MOST IN THIS JOB?

The opportunity to build a career with an established airline with a good reputation; the chance to work as part of a team and do something important that gives me satisfaction. I could use the skills I have developed and be sufficiently challenged to develop whilst learning from new people, processes and clients. I could then look forward to what opportunities my success in this role would bring.

IF YOU COULD, WHAT WOULD YOU CHANGE ABOUT THIS POSITION?

I relish the challenges that this position will provide and there's nothing I've seen that intimidates me in any way. By applying for this position, I have accepted everything that comes with it and therefore I would not change anything.

If pressed further mention turbulence.

HOW WOULD YOU APPROACH THIS ROLE?

I would approach this role with maturity, dedication and enthusiasm.

WHY SHOULD WE HIRE YOU INSTEAD OF SOMEONE WITH PRIOR CABIN CREW EXPERIENCE?

Although I might not have previous cabin crew experience, I have the necessary skills to make an impressive start and the willingness to learn and improve. Sometimes employers can do better when they hire people who don't have a great deal of repetitive experience. That way, they can train these employees in their methods and ways of doing the job. Training is much easier than un-training.

Or

I may not have had many years of experience in this field, but my knowledge and ability to learn quickly and work hard will enable me to make an immediate contribution to the job. With some specialised training and my desire to learn and improve myself, I could accomplish a lot in this position.

WHY SHOULD WE HIRE YOU FOR THIS POSITION RATHER THAN ANOTHER APPLICANT/I HAVE A PREFERRED CANDIDATE FOR THIS ROLE, CHANGE MY MIND.

I can't tell you why you should hire me instead of another candidate but, I can tell you why you should hire me.

WHY SHOULD WE HIRE YOU?

This job is exactly what I'm looking for, and I'm exactly what you are wanting. My skills and experience closely matches the major requirements and diverse responsibilities for this role. Plus I will bring a depth of practical knowledge and experience that will transfer well and benefit my performance as a cabin crew member, such as handling customer service issues, sales, working under pressure and communicating with different types of people.

Furthermore, I am an honest and upright person, who understands the need for high standards and rules. I refuse to compromise on standards and integrity. Within this, I can be relied upon to put the customer first and will always consider the needs of colleagues and of the organisation.

I'm driven to achieve, to surpass my most recent record, so you'll never see me deliver merely acceptable performance. I keep calm and don't let attention to detail slip when there is a lot of pressure and can be relied on to pull with the team when it's facing any kind of challenge.

I really think that the position could use someone with my attributes. XXX Airlines provide a fine service. I can offer top professionalism. Together we will make a winning team.

WHAT CHALLENGES DO YOU LOOK FORWARD TO?

An opportunity to apply my interpersonal skills in a new team, with a different set of customers and in a different environment.

WHAT DO YOU HOPE TO ACHIEVE FROM THIS POSITION/WHAT DO YOU WISH TO GAIN AT XXX AIRLINES?

I'd like to transfer all I've experienced to this airline, while at the same time having the opportunity to meet new challenges and achieve new goals.

WOULD YOU BE IN THE POSITION TO WORK OVERTIME IF REQUIRED?

Absolutely; I derive personal satisfaction from the extra effort that results in success. Extra effort makes the difference between a good job and a better one.

HOW IS YOUR WORK EXPERIENCE RELATED TO CABIN CREW/HOW HAS YOUR WORK EXPERIENCE PREPARED YOU FOR THE ROLE?

My work experience closely matches the requirements and diverse responsibilities of this position in many ways. For example,

Working as a hairdresser, I interact with a range of people on a daily basis and have to handle responsibility with a minimum of supervision. I am responsible for establishing and maintaining relationships with clients, dealing with customer service issues, sales, and admin. Furthermore, I am required to stand for long periods, work unsociable hours, pay attention to detail and be self starting with a lot of mental discipline.

My experience, I feel, will transfer well and enable me to make a significant contribution to this position and coupled with the training I will receive, I believe I will make an outstanding employee.

WHAT MAKES THIS JOB DIFFERENT FROM YOUR CURRENT/PREVIOUS ONES/ WHAT WAS THE LEAST RELEVANT JOB YOU HAVE HELD?

I really don't believe any two jobs are exactly the same, different customers, different projects and different approaches. However, there are more similarities than differences and if I focus on the similarities rather than the differences I will accomplish more and be contributing right from the start.

WHAT IS IT ABOUT BEING A CABIN CREW MEMBER THAT YOU THINK YOU DO NOT PRESENTLY HAVE?

From what I know about the position, I seem to have all the skills and experience required to make a thorough success. I don't believe that there are any areas that indicate gaps in my ability to do this job well and any gaps that may exist will be presented and filled during the 5 weeks training.

DO YOU FEEL READY FOR A MORE RESPONSIBLE POSITION/IN WHAT WAYS HAS YOUR WORK EXPERIENCE PREPARED YOU TO TAKE ON GREATER RESPONSIBILITY?

As I manage a business with real success I can certainly demonstrate that I can manage responsibility. I believe that 6 years experience working closely with customers, has prepared me professionally and personally to move up to this role. My customer care and teamwork skills have been finely tuned over the years and I know I am capable of greater achievements, which is why I'm interviewing for this position.

DO YOU FEEL CONFIDENT IN YOUR ABILITY TO HANDLE THIS POSITION?

Absolutely, I'm very confident in my abilities. I'm familiar with the basic job requirements and I learn quickly. It undoubtedly will take time and effort on my part, but I'm more than willing to devote that time and effort.

WHAT CHALLENGES DO YOU ANTICIPATE FROM THIS POSITION?

An opportunity to apply my interpersonal skills in a new team, with a different set of customers and in a different environment; the challenge will come from all those things.

DO YOU THINK YOUR LACK OF LANGUAGE SKILLS WILL AFFECT YOUR ABILITY TO PERFORM THE JOB?

I admit my language skills are a little light. However, should I be offered the position, I would be sure to increase my language abilities; I have a basic knowledge and understanding of conversational French, and would welcome the opportunity to further increase my fluency. I am also presently learning Spanish.

HOW DO YOU FEEL ABOUT WORKING AT CHRISTMAS, AND OTHER SPECIAL OCCASIONS?

I understand this from your job description and I considered this issue carefully before I applied, so it would not be a problem at all, I would be quite prepared to undertake this work when it is necessary.

WHAT WOULD YOU BRING TO THE POSITION//IN WHAT WAYS WILL XXX AIRLINES BENEFIT FROM HIRING YOU//I'M NOT SURE YOU ARE SUITABLE FOR THE POSITION, CONVINCE ME.

XXX Airlines would be getting someone whose skills and experience closely matches the major requirements and diverse responsibilities for this role. Plus I will bring a depth of practical knowledge and experience that will transfer well and benefit my performance as a cabin crew member, such as handling customer service issues, sales, working under pressure and communicating with different types of people.

Furthermore, I'm driven to achieve, to surpass my most recent record, so you'll never see me deliver merely acceptable performance. I am a hardworking member of the team and I keep calm and don't let attention to detail slip when there is a lot of pressure.

I have an outgoing personality and I pride myself on being able to build rapport quickly with new people. In fact, at Any Hair Salon, I was often asked to carry out the shampoo because the manager knew I would make the client feel welcome and important.

I really think that the position could use someone with my attributes. XXX Airlines provide a fine service. I can offer top professionalism. Together we will make a winning team.

WOULDN'T YOU MISS SPENDING TIME WITH YOUR FAMILY AND FRIENDS ON THESE SPECIAL OCCASIONS?

Naturally, I would miss spending time with my friends and family on these occasions, but my job and my career are as equally important to me as my friends and family and my family and friends respect that fact. Technology has made it possible for everyone to communicate easier which also helps.

THIS IS A LONG HOURS CULTURE, IS THAT A PROBLEM FOR YOU?

I understand that this a demanding job that I am applying for, but I really do thrive on the challenge of this sort of work and have worked long hours in the past– so I am willing to work whatever hours are necessary to get the work done.

HAVE YOU WORKED ON NIGHT SHIFTS BEFORE?

So far I haven't worked on a night shift. However, I have often worked long hours and evening shifts, so I could work a night shift without any problems.

HOW DO YOU FEEL ABOUT LIVING OUT OF A SUITCASE?

I don't have any concerns; I was aware of this fact before I applied for this position.

WOULD YOU BE WILLING TO TAKE A LIE DETECTOR TEST?

Yes. I have nothing to hide. If taking a lie detector test is a requirement of employment here, I'd first like to know the purpose and accuracy of the test.

WOULD YOU BE WILLING TO TAKE A DRUGS TEST/MEDICAL EXAMINATION?

Yes. I have nothing to hide and my health and physical wellbeing is excellent.

HOW DO YOU FEEL ABOUT A FORMAL DRESS CODE?

I have always liked to dress formally and feel very comfortable wearing suits. I realise that a standard of dress is necessary in order to project a positive image to the customers and general public.

HOW WILL YOU COPE WITH THE WIDE RANGE OF ETHNIC DIFFERENCES/HOW DO YOU FEEL ABOUT WORKING IN A VERY MULTI-CULTURAL ENVIRONMENT, COLLEAGUES AND CUSTOMERS?

I learnt about different cultures, customs and religions from a young age, through my years of education at school. I also have a cosmopolitan group of friends, so I feel comfortable with people who are from different ethnic backgrounds.

Any Hair Salon specialised in Afro Caribbean hairdressing and therefore attracted a large variety of people from many ethnic backgrounds. The manager and supervisor were both originally from Jamaica and spoke English as a second language. Not only did I have a good working relationship with them, we also became good friends.

These experiences will help me deal with all the different cultures I will encounter on a daily basis. If I am offered the position, I will also take steps towards enhancing my language skills to allow more flexibility.

HOW WILL YOU ADAPT YOUR BEHAVIOUR TO THE WIDE RANGE OF ETHNIC DIFFERENCES?

I will be careful about body language and gestures to ensure there are no misunderstandings, due to differentiations in meanings to different cultures.

If a language barrier exists, I will try to ensure that the passenger can understand my style of speech (pace, vocabulary or accent), by speaking slightly slower than usual, with clearer pronunciations. I will be careful to avoid slang, jargon, buzzwords, clichés, and colloquialisms and to further ensure that the passenger understands, I will make more use of facial expressions and hand gestures.

I never assume that they understand, I check for signs indicating a lack of comprehension, such as a vague or quizzical expression on the client's face, and a lack of response. If I feel that the client has not understood what I am trying to say, I am prepared to spend a little time to discuss it with them.

If I am offered the position, I will also take steps towards enhancing my language skills to allow more flexibility.

WHAT CONTRIBUTION CAN YOU MAKE TO ENSURE PASSENGERS WILL FLY WITH US AGAIN?

Service with a smile and a friendly, positive attitude will keep them loyal and keep them coming back.

A positive attitude to my work will not only ensure that the passengers enjoy their time with us; it will also help me by making my job easier, more interesting, more enjoyable and more rewarding.

GENERAL PERCEPTIONS

ON A SCALE OF 1 TO 10, WITH 10 BEING THE HIGHEST, HOW IMPORTANT IS WORK TO YOU?

9; Work is very important and is about more than the money. It's about having something meaningful to do, a reason to wake up in the morning, problems to solve, goals to accomplish, this is what life is all about to me.

As well as that though, it keeps me motivated, goal orientated and driven. Work can be very fulfilling, which makes me happy.

WHAT IS YOUR IDEA OF SUCCESS/DEFINE A SUCCESSFUL CAREER?

Success for me is about knowing that I have made a difference both to myself and my organisation. I like to make a difference to myself by developing my own skills. And I like to make a difference to my organisation by achieving good results.

Or

If I am successful, I will meet each new challenge with the confidence in my ability, yet will continue to be given new challenges that develop my abilities and make me even more productive.

WHAT PUBLIC FIGURES ARE YOUR ROLE MODELS?

I don't have a public role model, however I have had role models who I have personally known or worked with, such as my superiors at Any Hair Salon. Under their guidance, I grew personally and professionally.

My manager was a good role model and motivator. We had a very productive relationship and got along really well. She taught me many necessary skills and work methods and provided constant motivation and encouragement for my efforts. She was always full of good advice in a crisis and very generous with her time if anyone needed consoling. She could always make people laugh and was confident enough to be able to make fun of herself and her own mistakes. I consider myself very fortunate to have had her by my side early in my career, as a supervisor, teacher and remarkable person. She served as a role model for me and helped me develop my leadership and interpersonal skills.

I liked her as a person, respected her professionally, and appreciated her guidance.

HAS ANYONE IN THE BUSINESS WORLD EVER BEEN AN INSPIRATION TO YOU/WHO WAS THE MOST INFLUENTIAL PERSON IN YOUR LIFE?

Yes, several people. During my working life, I have been fortunate to have worked with some very skilled people who were exceptionally good at certain aspects of their role and who have influenced me. Through observation and discussion, I have identified what made them good at what they do and have tried to follow their examples. I think I've learned an even greater amount from these individuals than from text books I've read and the courses I've taken?

I have been most influenced by my manager at Any Hair Salon. From the time I began working at the salon, she took a sincere interest in my work, under her guidance, I grew personally and professionally. She expected a lot from me but gave a lot in return. She taught me many necessary skills and work methods and provided constant motivation and encouragement for my efforts. We always felt mutual respect and trust for each other. I consider myself very fortunate to have had her by my side early in my career, as a supervisor, teacher and remarkable person. She served as a role model for me and helped me develop my leadership and interpersonal skills.

PERCEPTIONS ABOUT CUSTOMER SERVICE

When answering these questions, it is important to bear in mind that there is a big difference between just delivering a product, and providing customer service. Successful candidates are likely to be those who understand that 'service' starts before boarding and ends after disembarkation. Candidates who think that the work ends once the last meal tray has been collected in will not progress very far!

HOW WOULD YOU DEFINE GOOD CUSTOMER SERVICE?

Good customer service is: Customer needs and expectations being met all of the time, every time throughout the life of the product or service. Without this, you have no customer loyalty.

WHAT IS THE KEY TO PROVIDING GOOD CUSTOMER SERVICE?

It's not enough to give good service: customers must perceive that they're getting good service. The key to success lies in full knowledge and understanding of the needs, expectations and attitudes of customers.

Or

Good customer care is about making people feel secure, relaxed and valued. This can be achieved by being friendly and approachable when accommodating the various needs of the customer, while showing empathy and interest.

WHEN HAVE YOU PROVIDED GOOD CUSTOMER SERVICE?

I provide good customer service every day; it is a necessary part of my job to ensure clients return. I take great pride in providing the best service I possibly can, and have never received any negative feedback.

A time when I have been particularly happy with the customer service I provided was when I was working at Any Hair Salon. I was in the staff room during my lunch break and I could hear a lot of noise coming from inside the salon. I went out to see what was happening and there were two young children who were there whilst their mum was having her hair done. The children were bored and not very happy; they were running around and constantly tugging at their mums coat asking to go home. I could sense that the situation was causing an inconvenience for not only the client but also the stylist.

I decided to go over and try to keep the children occupied. I sat them down and asked them if they would like to have their hair plaited. Their eyes lit up and they jumped at the chance. After finishing their hair, we sat down and made shiny bead bracelets from some hair beads. We had lots of fun and they really enjoyed themselves, which resulted in the client and the hair stylist having a stress free time.

The client was very thankful for my effort which was very rewarding. I felt really pleased that with just a little extra effort, I had made such a difference.

WHEN HAVE YOU THOUGHT THAT YOUR CUSTOMER SERVICE COULD HAVE BEEN BETTER?

I provide good customer service every day; it is a necessary part of my job to ensure clients return. I take great pride in providing the best service I possibly can, and have never received any negative feedback.

Not matter how much you are probed, do not give in.

WHEN HAVE YOU WITNESSED POOR CUSTOMER SERVICE/WHEN HAVE YOU WITNESSED GOOD CUSTOMER SERVICE?

I needed a particular material for a dress I was making. In most stores the salesperson would give me a quick 'no' before I finished explaining what I was looking for. Then in one store, I found a lady who waited patiently, giving me her undivided attention while I finished telling her what I wanted. She looked at me with a pleasant countenance, while she proceeded to explain why she didn't have the material I was asking for. She also made some helpful suggestions. As I looked at her, while she was talking to me, there was such sorrow in her voice that I actually began to feel sorry for the poor lady because she didn't have the material to sell me.

I didn't realise that she was taking it so seriously until I began to get sorry for her. I vowed, the next time I needed haberdashery supplies I would surely look to that lady.

WHAT DO YOU THINK CONSTITUTES POOR CUSTOMER SERVICE?

Major factors that contribute to poor customer service include job not done right, too slow, lack of courtesy, indifferent and unqualified personnel.

WHAT DO YOU FIND MOST CHALLENGING ABOUT PROVIDING CUSTOMER SERVICE?

The most challenging aspect is trying to keep everybody happy, the customer as well as the company. I enjoy the challenges of providing customer care. I think it's something I'm good at.

WHAT DO YOU MOST/LEAST ENJOY ABOUT PROVIDING CUSTOMER CARE?

The most enjoyable aspect I would have to say is that because I genuinely care about my client's satisfaction, it rewards me personally when I know that they are happy with the job I did, which in turn drives me to do better.

The least enjoyable aspect is when you have bent over backwards to provide good customer service, and nothing you do satisfies the customer. There are two sides to every situation so I take the rough with the smooth and make the best of each circumstance.

WHAT DO YOU THINK IS THE MAIN CAUSE OF SOME PASSENGER'S FRUSTRATIONS?

Common causes of irritation for passengers include flight delays, lost luggage, inadequate catering facilities and lack of space. Other causes may include incorrect, poorly displayed or missing information and poor service.

WHAT ASPECTS OF CUSTOMER SERVICE ARE MOST IMPORTANT TO OUR PASSENGERS?

People will return to a favourite airline not merely because the price, destinations, in-flight entertainment and food is good. Equally differential in their choice is the standard of service – passengers want to feel welcome, be entertained and amused while being looked after well and safely – whatever their needs, by people who are friendly, polite, approachable, willing to listen and professional, whatever the time of day and whatever the pressure. Passengers are most critical of an airline when they have been served in a rude or disinterested way.

Or

Anybody can fly you from A to B – that is the core product – but the standards of service, food and in-flight entertainment are vitally important, because, next to price, they are the main reason why customers make the choice they do.

WHY DO YOU THINK SOME PASSENGERS TAKE OUT THEIR FRUSTRATIONS ON CABIN CREW?

Cabin Crew wear the airlines uniform, and are therefore considered representative. This makes them a target for passengers to vent their frustrations upon.

HOW ARE YOU GOING TO COPE/HOW DO YOU THINK THIS WILL MAKE YOU FEEL?

I simply see it as part of the work. I will not take it personally because I know I am doing my job. I will remain calm, be professional and continue to offer the best service I can.

DO YOU THINK THE CUSTOMER IS ALWAYS RIGHT?

It depends on the situation. Whilst every customer is important, those who exhibit abusive behaviour or do anything to compromise safety are straying beyond the boundary. Therefore, the customer isn't always right.

HOW WOULD YOU DEAL WITH A PASSENGER WHO IS NOT RIGHT BUT BELIEVES HE IS RIGHT?

I would explain the company's rules and policies to the passenger in a calm, professional and positive manner. Hopefully, this should clarify any misconceptions that the passenger may have.

PERCEPTIONS ABOUT TEAMWORK & WORKING RELATIONSHIPS

HOW WOULD YOU DEFINE TEAMWORK?

The idea of teamwork is that a group of people who work in a coordinated way should be able to complete most tasks better and more effectively than the same group of people acting individually.

WHAT DO YOU THINK MAKES A CREW WORK WELL TOGETHER?

Essentially, a crew works well together when there is strong team commitment, open communication and good leadership.

They have respect for each other and the organisation they are part of, feelings are expressed freely and conflict is faced up and worked through.

Additionally, a team works well together when their intellectual and practical capabilities are challenged and put to the test, and some pressure is present. That gives them a sense of urgency of the job and stretches their faculties to the limit.

When all the above elements are met, it creates a feeling of camaraderie, and sometimes the team are able to inspire and motivate each other beyond even their own expectations.

WHAT DO YOU THINK PREVENTS A CREW WORKING WELL TOGETHER?

Teams may break down because lack of communication or poor leadership, or the root cause might be something relatively trivial like, clash of personalities, lack of motivation, and trust and sometimes training or ability is insufficient for the task.

SHOULD ANY OF THESE SITUATIONS OCCUR, HOW WOULD OR HAVE YOU DEALT WITH THE PROBLEM?

If there is lack of communication or leadership, I will take the initiative. If the problem is down to clash of personalities, I would act as a mediator, bringing the colleagues together and openly discussing the issue. It is very important for me to preserve neutrality, maintain integrity and project sincerity in those circumstances. If there is lack of motivation, I would challenge them to get something worthwhile done and nine times out of ten they will do it, and lack of training would require more training.

ARE YOU A GOOD TEAM PLAYER?

Yes I do consider myself a good team player because I am self motivated, I respect other people's opinions, I communicate well with my colleagues and I can be relied on to pull with the team.

WHAT IS YOUR DEFINITION OF A GOOD EMPLOYEE?

A good employee assumes responsibility, always works to the best of their abilities and is interested in improving. They communicate well and appropriately, feel and show team spirit, appreciate differences and show respect for others. They are also reliable and trustworthy and can appreciate criticism – not just tolerate or accept it, but benefit from it.

WHAT DO YOU ENJOY MOST ABOUT WORKING IN A TEAM?

The joy of working harmoniously with a group of people who are dedicated to something bigger than themselves, and are completely loyal to each other, counts in my experience as one of the most rewarding things in life. A new dimension is created when people work harmoniously together.

Nobody's perfect, but a team can be.

WHAT DO YOU LEAST ENJOY ABOUT WORKING AS PART OF A TEAM?

People not pulling their weight, is the least enjoyable aspect of working in a team, however I've noticed that such people simply lack enthusiasm and confidence, and that energetic and cheerful co workers can often change that, because enthusiasm is contagious.

WHAT DO YOU FIND MOST CHALLENGING ABOUT BEING PART OF A TEAM?

The most challenging aspect is inspiring and motivating other team members. Each has different needs and is motivated by different things.

WHAT ROLE WOULD YOU USUALLY ASSUME IN A TEAM SITUATION/ARE YOU A LEADER OR FOLLOWER? WHY?

I am both a leader and follower, if a situation comes up and someone has to take charge and I feel I can, then I will, but if a situation comes up and someone else has already taken charge and is solving it, I will follow. I am whatever I need to be.

WHAT DO YOU EXPECT FROM YOUR COLLEAGUES?

I expect from my colleagues what I expect from myself.

To value their own contribution, but not to the extent that it becomes more important than achieving the team objective, to be hard working, focused on quality customer care, honest and someone that others can rely upon.

WHAT DO YOU EXPECT FROM YOUR SUPERIORS?

I believe superiors should practice good management, lead by example and act as a positive role model. In addition, they should be secure in their ability to train, motivate, encourage and lead others.

HOW WILL YOU REACT IF YOUR COLLEAGUES OR SUPERIORS DO NOT MATCH UP TO YOUR EXPECTATIONS?

I would be very surprised if my expectations are not met because the criteria of people XXX Airlines look for. If it does occur however, I will not, under any circumstances, let it affect my professionalism or desire to do my best.

Or

I accept that my personal standards will sometimes be compromised, but they will not be permanently affected by the influence of others, or by circumstances, and I will still continue to do my best for the benefit of the passengers.

WHAT DO YOU THINK YOUR COLLEAGUES EXPECT OF YOU?

What I expect from my colleagues, they should and probably do expect from me. To value my own contribution, but not to the extent that it becomes more important than achieving the team objective, to be hard working, focused on quality customer care, honest and someone that others can rely upon.

WHAT KIND OF SUPERVISOR DO YOU LIKE TO WORK WITH/AROUND?

I enjoy working for anyone who practices good management and knows how to tap the potential of team members. The kinds who trust themselves and their employees to carry out their responsibilities – supervisors, who are secure in their ability to train, motivate, encourage and lead others. If the right employees are there, they will respond favourably. The result is a mature relationship with mutual respect where everyone succeeds and the company prospers.

WHAT QUALITIES OR BEHAVIOUR DO YOU LEAST LIKE IN A BOSS/LEADER/WHAT KIND OF SUPERVISOR DO YOU NOT LIKE TO WORK WITH/AROUND?

Although I can work with any leader, I would prefer to work with superiors who do not exhibit tendencies such as impatience, panic or being hypercritical.

HOW WILL YOU COPE IF A CREW MEMBER IN CHARGE HAS SOME OF THE QUALITIES/BEHAVIOURS YOU DISLIKE?

I accept that my personal standards will sometimes be compromised, and I will not, under any circumstances, let it affect my professionalism or desire to do my best.

However, if their behaviour interferes with my work, the first thing I do is watch and take notice if I've seen the behaviour in three other situations with the person. The reason for this is because the first two times are possibly chance but by the third time it's probably a pattern.

The second thing I would do is notice whether or not this person is dealing with a lot of stress. Stress may be causing this adverse behaviour and is not a regular occurrence. The third thing to do is to ask myself if I've been suffering from any exceptional stress. Stress on me may be causing me to see the world in a way that is contrary to what is actually going on.

The fourth: have I had an adult-to-adult conversation with this person? There are many times when the other person may or may not know that his/her behaviour is causing a problem for you and talking to him or her can clear up what turns out to be a simple misunderstanding. If that does nothing and the situation continues or worsens, I may then seek guidance from a higher source.

IN YOUR OPINION, WHAT MAKES THE BEST LEADER?

In my opinion, the best leader is skilled in the art of communication and is very much a people person who encourages cooperation between staff and acts decisively in a crisis or under pressure.

They act as a role model for the team members, by acting professionally at all times and maintaining standards by supporting the company's procedures and activities.

They have a keen sense of what is fair and deal with all people equally and justly.

WHAT QUALITIES DO YOU ADMIRE IN A GOOD LEADER?

I admire any leader who leads by example and acts as a positive role model for the team members. A leader who encourages cooperation between staff, acts decisively in a crisis or under pressure and has the ability to motivate and inspire confidence in others. These types of leaders usually win the confidence and respect of the entire team.

Other admirable attributes include: Recognising, using and showing appreciation for the skills of individual team members, accepting responsibility when things go wrong, duplicating skills in others, embracing both leader and follower and delegating while maintaining control.

WHAT MINIMUM QUALITY SHOULD A PERSON HAVE TO BE YOUR TEAM-MATE?

Although I can work with any person, I prefer to work with people who are honest because dishonest people are hard to trust and rely on.

HOW WILL YOU REACT IF YOU DO END UP WORKING WITH SOMEONE WHO IS DISHONEST?

I wouldn't let their actions prevent me from doing my best but, obviously I couldn't support a colleague who was behaving dishonestly either toward the company or with a customer.

HOW WOULD YOU DEFINE A GOOD WORKING RELATIONSHIP?

A good working relationship combines fairness, mutual respect and trust, openness and honesty in communication.

It is important that there is enough empathy and warmness towards colleagues but you should maintain just enough distance to be able to deal with problems that arise without being hampered by personal feelings.

WHAT DO YOU THINK IS AN IDEAL WORKING ENVIRONMENT?

The ideal work environment is a harmonious one, where team members work together towards a common goal and concentrate their efforts to get the job done in the shortest possible time. Their intellectual and practical capabilities are challenged and put to the test, and some pressure is present. That gives them a sense of urgency of the job and stretches their faculties to the limit. They have all equipment necessary to do the job, and undivided support from their superiors. That is the environment in which people improve in their jobs and achieve tangible results.

HOW WOULD YOU REACT IF THE IDEAL WORKING ENVIRONMENT IS NOT PRESENT?

No work environment is 100% perfect and to everyone's liking, so I would adapt and make the best of what I have.

DO YOU FEEL A SUPERVISOR AND EMPLOYEE SHOULD HAVE A STRICTLY BUSINESS RELATIONSHIP?

Socialising on one's own time depends on company policy and individual case.

My philosophy is that business and pleasure can be combined, but you have to set limits. There's a definite difference between being friendly with your co workers and working with friends. It's important to maintain just enough distance to be able to deal with problems that arise without being hampered by personal feelings. At work, there should always be a professional relationship in force.

HAS YOUR SOCIAL LIFE EVER INVOLVED ASSOCIATES OR CO WORKERS?

Some of my closest friends are also my ex co workers. We share the same interests and a similar lifestyle and feel close to each other, probably because of the close and productive relationships we had at work.

HOW DID YOU MANAGE TO MAINTAIN ENOUGH DISTANCE WITH YOUR COLLEAGUES AT ANY HAIR SALON?

At work, we always had a professional working relationship and worked well together.

WHAT WOULD YOU SAY ABOUT A SUPERVISOR WHO IS UNFAIR AND DIFFICULT TO WORK WITH?

The first thing I do is watch and take notice if I've seen the behaviour in three other situations with the superior. The reason for this is because the first two times are probably by chance, but by the third time it's probably a pattern.

The second thing I would do is notice whether or not this person is dealing with a lot of stress. Stress may be causing this adverse behaviour and is not a regular occurrence.

The third thing to do is to ask myself if I've been suffering from any exceptional stress. Stress on me may be causing me to see the world in a way that is contrary to what is actually going on.

The fourth: I would make an appointment to see the supervisor and have an adult to adult conversation. There are many times when the person may or may not know that his/her behaviour is causing a problem for you and talking to him or her can clear up what turns out to be a simple misunderstanding.

HOW WOULD YOU APPROACH THIS ADULT TO ADULT CONVERSATION?

I would enter the discussion in the frame of mind that we were equally responsible for whatever problems existed, and that this wasn't just the supervisor's problem. I would diplomatically explain that I feel uncomfortable in our professional relationship, that I feel he or she is not treating me as a professional, and therefore that I might not be performing up to standard in some way – I would ask for his or her input as to what I must do to create a professional relationship.

HOW DO YOU SHOW RESPECT FOR YOUR SUPERIORS?

Respect is very important to me. As an employee, I try to respect my superiors not only by following their guidance, but also seeking their guidance. When a trusting relationship is formed, I have often found that my superiors have appreciated concerns or opinions that I have raised to them. There is mutual respect.

HOW WOULD YOU DEFINE A CONDUCTIVE WORK ATMOSPHERE?

A conductive work atmosphere is a harmonious one, where the team has a genuine interest in its work and desire to deliver a good service.

HOW DO YOU DEAL WITH AUTHORITY?

I have no problems at all with authority. I like to know what my reporting line is and I realise that a big part of my job is satisfying the demands my superiors will make upon me.

DO YOU CRITICISE OTHERS AND UNDER WHAT CIRCUMSTANCES?

I don't really criticise, because I don't feel it is a constructive way to approach others, but I do try to offer constructive feedback. The circumstances would involve, when the objectives are not being met.

HOW DO YOU CRITICISE OTHERS?

I'm careful how I express my opinions; I never criticise in open forum. I gather my thoughts and formulate my ideas and then present them to the other person privately, that way you avoid belittling the other person.

I ensure the conversation focuses on any business discrepancies and does not get personal or spiral into blaming others. I also ensure that all feedback I give is as positive as possible so that the person on the receiving end thinks that any bad messages are balanced by their positive attributes and I always finish the conversation on a positive note.

WHAT IF YOUR OPINIONS ARE SOUGHT IN OPEN FORUM? I.E. A MEETING?

If opinions are sought in a meeting, I will give mine, although I am careful to be aware of others feelings.

HOW WOULD YOU HANDLE A TEAM MEMBER OR SENIOR CREW WHO MAKES A MISTAKE AND DOES NOT TAKE CRITICISM?

To soften the message, without losing its impact, I try to ensure that all feedback is as positive as possible. By ensuring that all feedback is as positive as possible, the person on the receiving end thinks that any bad messages are balanced by their positive attributes. It's much more likely that the feedback will be accepted – and appreciated that way.

DO YOU SPEAK UP IF YOUR OPINION DIFFERS FROM THAT OF OTHERS?

If my opinion differs from others, I put myself into their shoes and try to see it. Then I explain my opinions to them. In that process, the right solution is almost always found.

WHAT ACTION DO YOU TAKE IF YOU DISAGREE WITH THE DECISION OF YOUR MANAGER?

I would speak up. But there are times when tact is required – for example, if my manager were to say something in a meeting that I felt was wrong, I would wait until we had a moment alone to put my opinion across. At the end of the day though, I recognise that a manager is entitled to make decisions that I may not agree with. As long as I feel that I have been given a fair chance to air my views, I would have to go along with their decisions.

DO YOU TRY HARD TO GET PEOPLE (COLLEAGUES) TO LIKE YOU?

It is in my nature to try to get on with everyone I work with and I input a lot of effort into building trustworthy business relationships. If someone doesn't like me, I will see if there is anything I can do to change their perspective, but if I cannot, I will try to at least gain their respect so that we can continue to have a professional working relationship, where personal feelings do not interfere with the work.

Or

Good working relationships are essential to a successful career and to getting the work done, so I always try to earn the respect of others. If someone doesn't like me, I will see if there is anything I can do to change their perspective, but if I cannot, I will try to at least gain their respect so that we can continue to have a professional working relationship, where personal feelings do not interfere with the work.

HOW WOULD YOU TRY TO CHANGE THEIR PERSPECTIVE/GAIN THEIR RESPECT?

By continuing to be respectful and professional towards the other person, I would hope to change their perspective and/or establish their respect.

HOW IMPORTANT TO YOU IS THE AIM TO BUILD RELATIONSHIPS WITH CLIENTS, CO-WORKERS, PEERS AND MANAGEMENT?

To me, interaction between people is the most important factor in any business. The ability to work together as a team, absolute honesty with peers and customers, and a mutual feeling of trust and understanding, are essential for creating an efficient environment.

HAVE YOU SUCCESSFULLY WORKED WITH A DIFFICULT CO WORKER?

If by difficult you mean a person who is constantly complaining then yes I have; I remember one member of staff was always complaining, nothing was ever good enough or couldn't possibly work. Everyone had lost patience with her, but because she was so incredibly sensitive and really good at her job, no one said anything.

I spent some time with her and tactfully told her that it appeared as if she was always putting our ideas down. On hearing the feedback, she was genuinely horrified at her own behaviour. She explained that she hadn't realised it had made everyone feel that way and agreed that from then on, she would try to be more positive. Very quickly after that, we saw a change in her behaviour. She became more conscious of her own behaviour, deliberately trying to be more considerate. And from that point on, no one could have hoped for a more committed team member.

HAVE YOU EVER HAD DIFFICULTIES GETTING ALONG WITH OTHERS/TELL US ABOUT SOMEONE YOU HAVEN'T GOT ON WITH/HOW DID YOU DEAL WITH THE SITUATION?

I got on well with all my colleagues at Any Hair Salon. Naturally I was closer to some of my colleagues than with others, but we all got on well and worked well as a team.

Or

I remember one co-worker in particular who flat out didn't like me, it didn't matter what I did or said, or whether I tried to avoid or befriend this person. After a couple of days of subtle hostility, I decided to assert myself. I diplomatically explained that I acknowledged their personal dislike for me and drew upon the fact that we are both talented, dedicated and hardworking individuals and can therefore put aside our differences for the good of the salon, I asked for input as to what I must do to create a professional relationship. Although we never became friends, I was thereafter able to have pleasant exchanges with the person. I had bonded us in a novel way, under less than ideal circumstances.

WHAT WOULD YOU DO IF NO AMOUNT OF EFFORT ON YOUR PART SOLVED THE PROBLEM?

I would maintain cordial relations, but not go out of my way to seek more than a business like acquaintance. If nothing else, I always try to keep the channels of communication open by talking. Not speaking will not move either of us any further forward.

DO YOU PREFER TO WORK ALONE OR AS PART OF A TEAM/ DO YOU LIKE TO WORK IN A TEAM?

I am equally happy working alone or as part of a team and I am equally efficient in both. However, I prefer team spirit and the interactions between team members while working towards a common goal. In a team, people learn from each other and tend to achieve results faster, more efficiently and with greater satisfaction. The team approach to problem solving creates a harmonized work force and a more productive environment.

Or

Whilst I enjoy working in a team, I can work just as well and as hard alone. Though more pressure to produce might exist, it also proves to be a challenge.

Or

Whether I prefer to work as part of a team or alone depends on the best way to complete the job. Either way, I would work equally hard with the initiative required for success.

DO YOU LIKE TO WORK WITH PEOPLE?

Yes. I have always enjoyed the teamwork and interaction with my co-workers and customers.

WHAT IS THE DIFFERENCE BETWEEN COLLEAGUE AND FRIEND?

A colleague is a fellow member of a profession or association, someone with whom you work. A friend is a person with whom you have a personal relationship.

DESCRIBE YOUR IDEAL WORK GROUP.

My ideal work group would be one which has an infusion of character among the participants, where the members are able to inspire and motivate each other while retaining mutual trust and respect. There is open communication and good leadership and everyone is motivated to achieve a common aim. Decisions are made by consensus, feelings are expressed freely and conflict is faced up and worked through.

However, I understand that no work group is 100% perfect and to everyone's liking, so I adapt and make the best of what I have, while continuing to do my best for the benefit of the customers.

NAME THREE ADJECTIVES THAT BEST DESCRIBE YOUR IDEAL WORK COLLEAGUE/WHAT WOULD YOU LOOK FOR IN A COLLEAGUE?

It's difficult to think of an 'ideal' work colleague, however if I had to choose three adjectives I'd say: Communicative, honest and dependable.

WHAT TYPES OF PEOPLE DO YOU WORK WELL WITH/AROUND/WHAT TYPES OF PEOPLE DO YOU LIKE TO WORK WITH/AROUND?

I'd like to think I work well with most people, however, I prefer to work with people who can communicate effectively, are honest, dependable and nice in behaviour.

WHAT TYPES OF PEOPLE ARE YOU MOST COMFORTABLE WITH?

I am most comfortable with people who are honest, because dishonest people are hard to trust and rely on.

HOW WILL YOU REACT IF YOU DO END UP WORKING WITH SOMEONE WHO IS DISHONEST?

I wouldn't allow their behaviour to affect the way I work, but obviously I couldn't support a colleague who was behaving dishonestly either toward the company or with a client.

WHAT TYPES OF PEOPLE DO YOU NOT LIKE TO WORK WITH/AROUND?

I would say that I don't particularly enjoy working with people who display aggressive behaviour. People who are aggressive are often competitive; their goal is to win, which means that somebody else has to lose. This may be achieved by putting others down by overriding their feelings. Aggressive people attack as an immediate form of response; they often over react and in doing so hurt or humiliate the individuals they are dealing with.

But at the end of the day, it doesn't matter if I do not like who I work with, as long as the team objectives are met. I do not, under any circumstances, let it affect my professionalism or desire to do my best.

WHAT TYPES OF PEOPLE DO YOU FIND IT DIFFICULT TO WORK WITH/AROUND?

If I had to pick a type I find difficult, it would be people who use aggressive behaviour. The aggressive person expresses his or her feelings, needs and ideas at the expense of others. Aggressive people attack as an immediate form of response; they often over react and in doing so hurt or humiliate the individuals they are dealing with.

But at the end of the day, it doesn't matter if I do not like who I work with, as long as the team objectives are met. I do not, under any circumstances, let it affect my professionalism or desire to do my best.

WHAT BEHAVIOUR OF A PERSON DO YOU NOT LIKE/TELL US ABOUT SOMEONE YOU DISLIKE?

I do not like aggressive behaviour. The aggressor may shout at the people who fail to do all they demand, or it may be indirect and subversive, such as slipping in occasional put-downs until they rob people of their self confidence. They are both deadly and they are both bad behaviour.

But at the end of the day, it doesn't matter if I do not like who I work with, as long as the team objectives are met. I do not, under any circumstances, let it affect my professionalism or desire to do my best.

HOW WILL YOU DEAL WITH SOMEONE WHO POSSESSES THIS AGGRESSIVE BEHAVIOUR?

I would have an adult-to-adult conversation with the person. There are many times when the other person may or may not know that his/her behaviour is causing a problem and talking to him or her can clear up what turns out to be a simple misunderstanding.

If after the discussion, the behaviour continues or worsens, I will seek guidance and support from a superior in dealing with the situation.

HOW WOULD YOU APPROACH THE CONVERSATION?

I would approach the conversation in a calm, assertive and objective manner.

WHAT TYPES OF PEOPLE TRY YOUR PATIENCE?

Not much makes me impatient, however I understand that situations can occur occasionally, but instead of getting impatient, I exert my energy into maintaining my professional approach and conduct.

WHAT TYPES OF PEOPLE ANNOY YOU?

Usually I am not affected by annoying people. However I understand that situations can occur occasionally, but instead of getting annoyed, I exert my energy into maintaining my professional approach and conduct.

DO YOU HAVE DIFFICULTIES TOLERATING PEOPLE WITH DIFFERENT VIEWS OR INTERESTS THAN YOU?

No. I don't let the different views or interests of others affect how I feel about them. I judge them by the quality and quantity of their work. I get along with anyone whose accomplishments I can respect. Differing views and personalities add richness to a team; after all you don't want a team of clones.

THIS JOB WILL REQUIRE YOU TO WORK WITH PEOPLE FROM VERY DIFFERENT BACKGROUNDS TO YOURSELF – HOW WILL YOU COPE?

I worked with people from different backgrounds while I was working at Any Hair Salon. Both the manager and supervisor were originally from Jamaica and spoke English as a second language and many of my other colleagues were much more highly qualified than myself, but not only did I have a good working relationship with these people, we also became good friends.

Based on this past experience, I believe I will cope fine.

HOW WILL YOU COPE WITH THE WIDE RANGE OF PERSONALITIES AMONG OUR EMPLOYEES?

The same way I have coped in the past. Working at Any Hair Salon, I worked with people who had very different personalities. Some of them had loud, exuberant personalities whilst others were sensitive and quiet. I understand that a range of personalities exist in any workplace and I observe and respect each of them accordingly.

DO YOU THINK YOU CAN GET ALONG WITH X PERSONALITY?

I don't let the personalities of others affect how I feel about them. I judge them by the quality and quantity of their work. I get along with anyone whose accomplishments I can respect.

HOW DO YOU GET ALONG WITH DIFFERENT KINDS OF PEOPLE?

Dealing with people is something I really enjoy. I like contact with colleagues and clients and would generally describe myself as a sociable person. I have very good interpersonal skills and I pride myself on being able to build rapport quickly with new people. To me, establishing rapport seems to be a natural tendency. In fact, at Any Hair Salon, I was often asked to carry out the shampoo because the manager knew I would make the clients feel welcome and important.

HOW DO YOU MAKE CLIENTS FEEL WELCOME AND IMPORTANT?

I make them feel welcome and important by making them feel comfortable, relaxed and valued.

WHAT IS MOST IMPORTANT IN THE WORKPLACE, TOTAL HONESTY, OR SUPPORTIVENESS TOWARDS COLLEAGUES?

I think honesty and supportiveness are both important, but obviously I couldn't support a colleague who was behaving dishonestly either toward the company or with a client.

HOW DO YOU SHOW INTEREST IN YOUR CO WORKERS/HOW DO YOU GO ABOUT ESTABLISHING RAPPORT AND TRUST/HOW WILL YOU ESTABLISH A WORKING RELATIONSHIP WITH OUR EMPLOYEES?

To me, establishing rapport seems to be a natural tendency. The greatest part is often established non-verbally. By being empathetic, treating people with respect and being willing to listen and help, I create a feeling of trust and confidence in my team mates.

Matching my behaviour to suit the particular situation or person also helps in the process. Matching voice tone or tempo to that of the person I'm talking to, controlling body language, posture and gesture is also important.

Taking a genuine interest in other people, being curious about who they are and how they think and being willing to see the world from their point of view also makes them more receptive.

All this is done almost automatically and naturally. I consider myself lucky for not having any problems in establishing rapport with others.

HAVE YOU EVER WORKED FOR A SUPERIOR WHO WAS YOUNGER OR LESS EXPERIENCED THAN YOURSELF?

I haven't worked for such a superior. My former superiors were very experienced professionals who were older than myself, from whom I've learned a lot. I don't consider age so important, what matters is a person's credibility, professionalism and competency.

HOW WILL YOU COPE BEING SUPERVISED BY SOMEONE YOUNGER OR VERY MUCH OLDER THAN YOURSELF?

I am comfortable working with any age group. I am far more interested in their qualities as a supervisor than in their age.

Or

I don't consider age so important, what matters is a person's credibility, professionalism and competency.

Or

I think it can be highly beneficial to have a mix of ages and types of experience – it provides a good opportunity for learning.

ARE YOU ABLE TO WORK ALONE WITHOUT DIRECT SUPERVISION?

Owing to the nature of my occupation and the kind of tasks that I carry out in my job, I work independently on a regular basis. I am a self starter and don't need constant reassurance. I can set my own goals, or I can take assigned goals and complete them. I'm inner directed and enjoy applying my creativity and problem solving skills to my work. However, I'm not one of those individuals who will keep doing something wrong rather than seeking help. It's better to ask twice than loose your way once.

HYPOTHETICAL QUESTIONS

These kind of questions present candidates with difficult 'real-life' situations, where almost any answer can be challenged. Bear in mind: if you are not cabin crew yet, you cannot really be expected to know the best reply - so do not be tricked into entering into an argument with an interviewer! A good way to approach these questions is to consider the feelings of all involved - and think about the implications for your colleagues and the airline as well.

Prove to your recruiters that you would be 'proactive' and do you best to resolve the situation using your own initiative - whilst remembering that you could ask for the help of more experienced crew if necessary. If you have followed these guidelines, and are still challenged, your interviewer may be testing your ability to manage conflict or stress. In either case it is important to remain calm, focused, and to demonstrate that although you appreciate there are many aspects to each situation, you would always be trying to find acceptable solutions.

WHAT WOULD YOU DO IF A COMMERCIALLY IMPORTANT PASSENGER COMPLAINED ABOUT A CRYING CHILD?

I would apologise to the passenger and offer my assistance to the guardian of the crying child. I would be proactive and do my best to resolve the situation using my own initiative – whilst remembering that I can ask for the help of more experienced crew if necessary.

IF YOU WERE GIVEN THE JOB OF INTERVIEWING CABIN CREW FOR XXX AIRLINES, HOW WOULD YOU DO IT?

If I had the job of picking cabin crew, I would look for desirable traits such as:

An approachable and friendly personality

Teamwork and customer care skills

Good communication and admin skills

An ability to work under pressure

A spirit of enthusiasm, confidence and a sense of humour.

The ability to manage change and adversity

Good listener and problem solver

These are the qualities I feel are necessary for the position.

WHAT WOULD YOU DO IF YOU SUSPECT THAT A PASSENGER IS SUSPICIOUS OR A HIGH RISK TO PASSENGERS?

I would report to the senior any abnormal behaviour, indicating a suspicious passenger.

WHAT DO YOU CONSIDER SUSPICIOUS BEHAVIOUR?

I consider someone who is fidgety, constantly looking around and being anxious to be suspicious behaviour.

WHAT WOULD YOU DO AND HOW WOULD YOU REACT IN A HIJACKING?

I'm sure there is a corporate policy for dealing with this situation and I will follow it.

HOW WOULD YOU HANDLE A COLLEAGUE WHO IS BEING RUDE, RACIST, ETC.?

If there is a corporate policy, I will follow it, if not; I will warn the person the first time and make it clear that this sort of behaviour is not on. If he or she continues, I would then report it to proper authority.

IF YOU SPOTTED A COLLEAGUE DOING SOMETHING UNETHICAL OR ILLEGAL, WHAT WOULD YOU DO?

I would act immediately to put a stop to any unethical or illegal activity. I would try to document the details of the incident and try to collect any physical evidence. Then I would report it to my senior.

WHAT THREE ITEMS WOULD YOU CHOOSE TO HAVE IF TRAPPED ON A DESERT ISLAND?

The 3 items I would have to have would be a medical kit containing various medicines, water purification tablets, surgical blades, plasters and cotton wool, etc. Second, I would have my survival kit containing essential items such as a compass, a striker and flint, a torch, waterproof matches, tallow candles (for eating, melting and frying), a magnifying glass, fish hooks and line. Third, A survival pouch containing fuel tablets, flexible saw, signal flares, a radio transmitter, brew kit and food.

Each 3 items are light-weight, conveniently small and can enable you to deal with a multitude of tasks.

IF YOU WERE TRAPPED ON A DESERT ISLAND, WHAT BOOK WOULD YOU WANT AND WHY?

I would have to have my pocket sized 'Collins Gem, SAS survival guide', by John Wiseman. The guide is packed full of practical advice on survival in the wild, containing everything from attracting attention to yourself so that rescuers may find you to making your way across unknown territory back to civilisation if there is no hope of rescue.

There is essential information about navigating without a map or compass, maintaining your morale and that of others who share your situation, what to eat, how to take everything possible from nature and use it to the full, and how to maintain a healthy physical condition, or if sick or wounded heal yourself and others.

IF YOU WERE GOING TO MARS, WHAT 3 ITEMS WOULD YOU TAKE?

First, an expert in the field. Second, sufficient oxygen to allow me to breathe in that environment. And finally, enough fuel for the return trip.

WHAT WOULD YOU DO IF YOU RECEIVED A TELEPHONE CALL TELLING YOU THAT A FAMILY MEMBER HAS BEEN TAKEN ILL IN THE MIDDLE OF THE DAY?

I would ring home, at the earliest convenience, to find out what the situation was. If it was something extremely serious (life or death situation), then I would hope that my employer would understand the need for me to take time off work at the earliest convenience. If on the other hand, the situation were not so serious, I would continue with my work as necessary.

WHAT WOULD YOU DO IF THE SEAT BELT SIGNS ARE ON BECAUSE OF TURBULENCE, BUT A PASSENGER GETS UP TO GO DESPERATELY TO THE TOILET?

That is a new area for me, so I am afraid I can't really answer that, but I enjoy acquiring new knowledge and I do learn quickly.

Or

I'm sure there is a corporate policy for dealing with this situation and I will follow it.

Or

In non fatal accidents, turbulence is the biggest cause of injuries to both passengers and crew. Therefore I would suggest that the passenger wait until the seatbelt signs are turned off. If the passenger really cannot wait, I may seek the advice of a senior member of crew.

YOU ARE IN A TEAM OF 4 AND YOU ARE GIVEN HALF THE WORK, WHAT DO YOU DO?

It depends on the circumstances, if I feel that my supervisor thinks I am the only person who can do the job, I will do it. Normally, if I can finish the work within the allocated time, I will not complain, otherwise I will let my supervisor know and if he/she still insists on me doing it, I will do it.

YOU ARE IN A TEAM OF 4 AND YOU ARE ONLY GIVEN AN EIGHTH OF THE WORK, WHAT DO YOU DO?

If I feel my supervisor did not give me more work because he does not have the confidence in me, I will talk to him and do something to improve his confidence. In all other cases, once I finish my work, I will let my supervisor know that I can take a new assignment.

YOU HAVE A DEADLINE AND NO TIME, BUT A TEAM MATE NEEDS HELP, WHAT DO YOU DO?

If the situation is an easy one and not time consuming, then I will help, otherwise I will ask him to wait until I finish my task and then help him.

YOU ARE IN FLIGHT AT 30,000 FEET, HOW WOULD YOU HANDLE A PASSENGER IF HE BECAME IRATE ABOUT HIS LOST BAGGAGE?

At 30,000 feet, there is not a lot you can do about the baggage so, the problem at hand is reassuring the passenger and avoiding further disruption. First, I would manoeuvre the passenger somewhere more private and sit him down, if possible. I would then ask him to quietly tell me about the situation, I would then apologise for the mishandling and offer to assist on the ground by escorting him to the proper people who can help.

YOU HAVE A DOCTORS APPOINTMENT ARRANGED, YOU HAVE WAITED 2 WEEKS TO GET IT, AN URGENT MEETING IS SCHEDULED AT THE LAST MOMENT, WHAT DO YOU DO?

If it is not a life or death situation, then I would reschedule the appointment. I would then make sure I was properly prepared for the meeting.

HOW WOULD YOU ACT IN AN EMERGENCY/HOW DO YOU DEAL WITH A CRISIS?

I treat a crisis like a crisis. I move quickly, confidently, and authoritatively in those situations where decisive action is required.

WHAT IS THE DEFINITION OF AN EMERGENCY?

An emergency is 'when something unexpected happens that requires major decisions to be made, quickly.'

HOW WOULD YOU ACT IN AN EMERGENCY SUCH AS A CRASH LANDING?

As soon as I get the warning that something is going to happen, I would get a plan together in my mind. I would stay calm and in control and follow the emergency guidelines and procedures.

HOW WOULD YOU HANDLE A PASSENGER WHO IS INTOXICATED?

I would not provide any more alcoholic drinks; I would encourage food and offer a cup of tea or coffee. If the situation does not improve but instead worsens and the situation is out of my control, I would inform my senior and seek assistance from the other crew members.

WHAT WOULD YOU DO IF YOU FELT YOUR SUPERIOR WAS DISHONEST/INCOMPETENT/HAD A PERSONAL PROBLEM?

That would depend on the seriousness of the problem and whether or not it was affecting his ability to do his job. Obviously in the case of dishonesty or incompetence, action would be required. A personal problem might or might not affect others in the workplace and I would need to make a judgement on the individual case.

WHAT ACTION WOULD YOU TAKE IF THE PROBLEM WAS AFFECTING HIS ABILITY TO DO HIS JOB OR OTHERS ABILITY TO DO THEIRS?

Only if the problem was that serious, I would report it to someone who could correct and rectify the situation.

WHAT IF I TOLD YOU THAT YOUR PRESENTATION THIS AFTERNOON WAS LOUSY?

First of all, I would ask which aspects of my presentation were lousy. My next step would be to find out where you felt the problem was. If there was miscommunication, I'd clear it up. If the problem was elsewhere, I would seek your advice and be sure that the problem was not recurrent.

HOW WOULD YOU DEAL WITH A PASSENGER WHO IS SCARED OF FLYING?

I would go down to their level by kneeling next to where they are sitting, I would reassure the passenger that I understand and talk softly and calmly, talking them through the flight and reassuring them of any strange noises they may hear.

Being aware of what to expect will help keep those worries in check. Just realising that a planes wings are supposed to flex, to move around gently in flight, can help. Similarly, the collection of bumps and bangs that always accompany flight can be made less fearsome if they are expected. I would tell them where I can be found and show them the call bell. And finally say I will check on them during the flight

YOU ARE IN A TEAM, AND ALL THE MEMBERS WANT TO SOLVE A PROJECT IN A CERTAIN WAY, HOWEVER YOU KNOW A BETTER WAY TO SOLVE THE PROBLEM, WHAT DO YOU DO?

In this situation, you run the risk of people, especially those who may have championed the strategy, not appreciating your input. I would raise my suggestions in a vulnerable and respectful, yet assertive way by saying something along the lines of, "this is just a suggestion, but one that I think everyone ought to consider". If necessary, I would talk to members on an individual basis (the leader first) to discuss the idea and illustrate some examples to gain as much support as possible.

WHAT WOULD YOU DO IF NO AMOUNT OF EFFORT ON YOUR PART PERSUADED THE OTHER TEAM MEMBERS?

Although I may not agree, I would go along with what the leader decides.

WHAT DO YOU DO WHEN A COLLEAGUE COMES TO YOU IN TEARS?

Naturally, I would take them aside and figure out what it was that was upsetting them so. If it were something that I could help with – for example getting them over a difficult deadline – I would try to offer them my time. But if it was a personal problem, I would try to listen and offer my support and shoulder to cry on.

HOW DO YOU DEAL WITH LAZY PEOPLE?

It takes a lot of energy to be lazy, keep a job and not get caught. It needs planning, forethought, charm, effort, energy, determination, intelligence, originality, guile and judgement: all the things needed for success and to be a five star employee. Perhaps there are no lazy staff, just bad bosses?

WHAT DO YOU DO WHEN A CO-WORKER IS NOT PULLING THEIR WEIGHT?

I've noticed that such people simply lack enthusiasm and confidence, and that energetic and cheerful co workers can often change that. So when I feel others are not pulling their weight, I first try to overcome it with a positive attitude that I hope will catch on, if this does nothing, I will try to reason with and challenge the person. Failing that, I will need to consider seeking advice from a senior member of staff.

TECHNICAL QUESTIONS

Career Goals & Future Progression

About the Airline

In this context 'technical' questions are defined as those that have clear and factual answers. They reveal very little about personal qualities, except that a candidate has made the effort to find something out about the airline or plan their future.

It would be a good idea to do some basic research, and find out who the airline's chairman is, the history of the airline, the destinations operated, awards won and any recent initiatives (especially if they have been advertised, or have appeared in the news).

CAREER GOALS AND FUTURE PROGRESSION

HOW DID YOU BECOME INTERESTED IN THE POSITION OF CABIN CREW/THE TRAVEL INDUSTRY?

I have always been interested in cabin crew, in anything to do with travel really. I grew up around aviation, my father worked at Any Aerospace and because of his work, we lived very close to the airport. This is where my passion for flying initially started. But it wasn't until I carried out a career suitability test at school that I really started to consider cabin crew as a serious future prospect. The test examined personal attributes, goals and skills and the final result came back suggesting suitability for the occupation. Based on this, I done a little more research into the job and agreed. This seems to be a job for which I am suited and is one I will feel committed to. I believe I can make the best contribution to a company by being happy at what I do.

WHY DO YOU WANT TO BE A CABIN CREW MEMBER/WHY WOULD YOU BE HAPPY DOING THIS TYPE OF WORK?

Besides the fact that being a member of Cabin Crew has always been a lifelong ambition of mine, being a member of Cabin Crew also offers everything I'm looking for, both in the position itself and in the overall environment.

I want a job that offers not the normal nine to five, but something which is more varied, that allows me to contribute in different areas and work and meet with a wider range of people and cultures.

Being a member of cabin crew, I could use the customer care skills I have developed over the course of my career to deliver the standard of service that passengers expect and be sufficiently challenged to develop further whilst learning from new people, processes and clients.

I feel that for the above reasons I would be successful as cabin crew and would be a valuable asset to XXX Airlines.

HAVE YOU APPLIED FOR ANY OTHER POSITIONS?

At this stage, the position of cabin crew is the only position of interest that fits both my skills and career aspirations.

HOW WILL YOU ADAPT TO RETURNING TO FULL TIME EMPLOYMENT AFTER WORKING INDEPENDENTLY?

Being cabin crew is something I've always wanted to do and I have prepared myself for the transition. I enjoy the challenge of learning about and adapting to a new environment. That's one of the reasons I am seeking to make a change right now. I do not anticipate any problems adapting.

HOW HAVE YOU PREPARED YOURSELF FOR THE TRANSITION?

I have prepared myself through the research I have done, the skills and experience I have acquired.

CAN WE TAKE IT THEN THAT YOU DO STILL WISH US TO CONSIDER YOU FOR THIS POST?

Certainly! Having had this chance to meet you and learn more about your operation and what the post will entail, I am even keener than before. I am convinced that this is the opportunity I am seeking and I know I can make a contribution.

WOULD YOU TAKE THIS JOB IF WE OFFERED IT TO YOU?

Yes, definitely. I was keen as soon as I saw the job opening on the web site. More than that though, actually meeting potential colleagues and finding out more about your current activities has clarified still further what an exciting challenge it would be to work here.

WHEN ARE YOU AVAILABLE TO START WORK IF OFFERED THE POSITION?

I have the energy and enthusiasm to start straight away. All I need is a weeks notice and I'm ready.

WHAT WOULD YOU SAY IF I SAID YOUR SKILLS AND EXPERIENCE WERE BELOW THE REQUIREMENTS OF THIS JOB?

I would ask what particular aspects of my skills and experience you felt were lacking and address each one of those areas with examples of where my skills and experiences do match your requirements. I would expect that after this discussion you would be left in no doubt about my ability to do this job.

IF YOU WERE TO LEAVE THE FLIGHT DEPARTMENT, WHERE WOULD YOU TURN YOUR SKILLS?

If for any reason, I was to leave the flight department, I would turn my skills to cabin crew training, or possibly airport personnel.

HOW WOULD YOU RESPOND IF WE TOLD YOU THAT YOU HAVE BEEN UNSUCCESSFUL ON THIS OCCASION/HOW WOULD YOU FEEL AND WHAT WOULD YOU DO IF DIDN'T SECURE A POSITION WITH US TODAY?

Naturally it will be a disappointment if I do not secure this job today because it is something I really want, I feel ready for it and I have had plenty of experience to contribute. However, I am not one to give up quickly; I will think about where I went wrong and how I could have done better, at the same time, I would take steps towards strengthening my candidacy.

HOW LONG HAVE YOU BEEN LOOKING FOR A NEW POSITION?

I have only recently started looking for a new position; this is my first application and interview.

WHY HAVE YOU DECIDED TO CHANGE PROFESSIONS AT THIS STAGE OF YOUR CAREER?

This career turnaround hasn't come suddenly. I have always liked this profession and have been gradually mastering the skills needed to perform its tasks. I am now ready to assume the responsibility and start achieving results.

HOW DO YOU FEEL ABOUT LOOKING FOR ANOTHER JOB?

Looking for another job is an opportunity. I don't have to be looking for another job; I do it so that I can continue to grow professionally.

HOW IMPORTANT IS JOB SECURITY TO YOU?

Security is a basic need, but I know that there are no guarantees in life. The only true job security comes from making a meaningful contribution to my employer. If I know my job will be around for as long as I excel at it, I am able to concentrate on my work and remain focused.

HOW LONG WOULD YOU STAY WITH US?

I'm a loyal sort of person, and I don't like changing more than I need to. If the job is as challenging as I'm sure it is, and the opportunities for development within your organisation are as good as I believe they are, it may well be a career long commitment.

Or

I approach every new job with a long-term view. I would like to think that I can make a positive contribution to XXX Airlines for the foreseeable future.

WHEN DO YOU EXPECT A PROMOTION/WHAT DO YOU THINK DETERMINES PROGRESS?

That depends on a few criteria. Of course, I cannot expect a promotion without the performance that marks me as deserving the promotion. I would like my career to continue progressing as well as it has in the past, but I'm a realist. I know promotions aren't given, they're earned. When I've mastered the position, improved it with my ideas, and prepared myself to take on new responsibilities, I'll be ready for a promotion.

HOW IMPORTANT TO YOU IS THE OPPORTUNITY TO REACH THE TOP?

Reaching the top is a very relative term, but if by reaching the top you mean being a top performer and being successful in my occupation, I do consider reaching the top as very important.

HOW MUCH THOUGHT HAVE YOU GIVEN TO YOUR FUTURE?

Essentially, I have given my career and opportunities a great deal of thought, but business changes so rapidly these days, it's hard to plan precisely. But I do know I want to get ahead in the airline industry and I think the opportunities to do that in this airline are excellent.

WHERE DO YOU PICTURE YOURSELF IN 5 YEARS/WHAT ARE YOUR LONG TERM CAREER OBJECTIVES?

This is a lively and expanding company by all accounts, so I very much hope that I shall be here in 5 years time. My job will have increased at least one possibly two levels in responsibility and scope and I'll have become a thorough professional with a clear understanding of the industry and company. I'll have made a significant contribution and will be working on new ways to further my career. By this time, my goals for the long term should be sharply defined.

SO YOU DON'T YET HAVE ANY LONG TERM PLANS?

I'm certainly ambitious, and I like to keep moving and progressing, but I find it's far more rewarding to let the job lead me forward.

WHAT GOALS DO YOU HAVE?

My general goal is to do everything possible to keep learning and expanding my knowledge and skills. Beyond that, my goal is to maintain optimum health through exercise and a proper diet.

HOW WILL THIS JOB HELP YOU REACH YOUR CAREER GOALS?

I am consistently striving to increase my knowledge and skills and I believe that this position can offer me a real step up in terms of challenge and experience. I feel that my present career plans would be more than fulfilled by this role. The position would allow me to use the skills I already have, but be sufficiently challenging to give the opportunity for further development.

WHAT STEPS HAVE YOU ALREADY TAKEN TO ACHIEVE YOUR GOALS?

One of the most significant steps I've taken is applying for this job. The position could be significant for my future development, experience and knowledge.

WOULD YOU LIKE TO HAVE MY JOB?

Only for the next ten minutes so that I could hire myself.

ARE YOU'RE PRESENT CAREER OBJECTIVES DIFFERENT FROM YOUR ORIGINAL GOALS?

No; I have always wanted to get into this profession and through all the positions I have worked, I have been gradually mastering the skills needed to perform its tasks. I am now ready to assume the responsibility and start achieving results.

DESCRIBE THE PERFECT JOB/WHAT WOULD YOU CONSIDER TO BE THE IDEAL JOB FOR YOU?

The perfect job is one that offers daily challenges, provides the kind of stimulation that keeps my skills and abilities at peak levels, and allows me to achieve tangible results on a regular basis – something that is fast paced, in a situation where new ideas and creativity are fostered.

WHAT DO YOU WANT OUT OF YOUR LIFE?

I want a successful career, personal development and good health.

SO YOU WOULDN'T LIKE AN EASY LIFE, WHERE YOU DIDN'T NEED TO WORK/WOULD YOU WORK IF YOU SUDDENLY BECAME A MILLIONAIRE/WHY DO YOU WORK?

I don't have any desire for an easy life. I suppose an easy life would be nice for a while, but then I would become restless. I'm interested in achievement, accomplishment, and seeing just how much I can do with the talent and intelligence I have. My career remains my first priority.

Or

Working is about more than the money, it's about having something meaningful to do, a reason to wake up in the morning, problems to solve, goals to accomplish, this is what life is all about to me. I suppose a life of luxury would be nice for a while, but then I would become restless. My career remains my first priority.

WHEN DO YOU PLAN TO RETIRE/WHAT WILL YOU DO IN YOUR RETIREMENT?

Retirement is not something that I have thought a great deal about. I have many goals to achieve and so my plans for retirement will come later in my career.

ABOUT THE AIRLINE

HAVE YOU EVER FLOWN WITH XXX AIRLINES/ WHAT DO YOU THINK ABOUT THE WAY WE RUN OUR OPERATION?

I flew with XXX Airlines from London to California in October 2004. I had always heard so many wonderful things about the airline and had to try you out.

Onboard, the service was excellent and I felt like I was flying first class. The meal was outstanding, about the best you'll find anywhere ... The seats were comfortable and the in-flight entertainment was impressive, with a variety to choose from.

As for the crew, they really take care of all their passengers and they do everything to make the flight as pleasant as possible. They are attentive, competent and very friendly and fun to talk to, and always smiling.

XXX Airlines really are a classy airline and deserve to be the best airline in the world.

WHAT IS THE WORST THING YOU HAVE HEARD ABOUT XXX AIRLINES?

The worst thing I have heard about this organisation is that competition for jobs is fierce because it is a terrific company. Every thing else I have heard, have been impressively positive.

HOW LONG WOULD IT TAKE YOU TO MAKE A CONTRIBUTION TO XXX AIRLINES?

I would predict that I will make an immediate contribution to XXX Airlines. Training is a factor and it takes time to learn, but it's not necessary to wait until after training has been completed to make a contribution.

WHAT ARE YOUR FEELINGS ABOUT A MEDIUM SIZED AIRLINE?

Medium sized companies have emerged from their growing pains and are more secure in their markets than smaller companies. Yet, they haven't become large and impersonal; they are still able to respond quickly to change. I like the potential for being involved in even more growth with the company.

WHAT ARE YOUR FEELINGS ABOUT A LARGE AIRLINE?

I welcome the opportunity to work in a large, developed, well known airline such as this. The resources and potential for advancement in a large organisation are not available in smaller companies. I'd be proud to add my skills and abilities to the excellence that flourishes here.

WHAT IS YOUR ATTITUDE TOWARDS WORKING IN A SMALL AIRLINE?

Most innovative, energetic and highly competitive companies are not big in size. I have always valued highly the participation of employees in the decision making process and the family feeling of the small company, where team spirit, daily challenges and hands on involvement in solving business problems bring a sense of achievement and a quick response to changes and new opportunities.

WOULD YOU PREFER TO WORK FOR A LARGE, MEDIUM OR SMALL AIRLNE?

I am equally happy; I do not have a preference either way. It is more important for me to enjoy working for the airline and feel a part of the team.

WHY DO YOU WANT TO WORK FOR XXX AIRLINES/WHAT INTERESTS YOU MOST ABOUT XXX AIRLINES/WHY DID YOU SELECT XXX AIRLINES?

The safety record and outstanding reputation of XXX Airlines was a significant factor that influenced my decision to apply. When people think of XXX Airlines, they know what they are getting – a consistently high and reliable service and an airline that cares about their customers, this fact is also demonstrated by the many awards that the airline has received.

Also, I have flown with XXX Airlines in the past and was very impressed with the service I received. As well as projecting an excellent image, I see a vibrant, responsive organisation with great potential for growth, and I want to be part of it.

I know that I'll be able to contribute to the airlines future success.

DO YOU HAVE ANY RESERVATIONS ABOUT WORKING HERE?

I see this position as a fine opportunity and the airline as one I would be proud to be a member of. I don't have any reservations at this point and I wouldn't be applying to join you if I did.

IF ONE OF OUR COMPETITORS OFFERED YOU A JOB NOW, WOULD YOU TAKE IT?

Because I want to work as cabin crew, if I did not get this job with XXX Airlines, then I would have to consider other airlines. However, XXX Airlines are my first and best choice.

HOW WOULD YOU DESCRIBE THE IDEAL AIRLINE?

The ideal airline is a progressive, forward-thinking one that provides a challenging, stimulating and supporting atmosphere for its employees and their achievements. People enjoy working there and give their best to achieve the company's goals and targets.

HAVE YOU APPLIED TO ANY OTHER AIRLINES?

I have researched other airlines that would interest me but, after researching the history, development and future plans of XXX Airlines, along with meeting people who work here, it seems like a perfect fit. I really appreciate what XXX Airlines has to offer in the way of growth potential, and good reputation and I would really like to work for you, so although it is taking a bit of a risk, I wanted to see how things went with my application to you, before I considered applying to any other airlines.

Or

Although I am set on making cabin crew my future career, making a job change is a major decision, a long term commitment that I take very seriously, therefore the job I take, and the people I work with have got to have values that I can identify with. I'm very choosy about the airlines I approach and have not found such an interesting airline as this so far.

HOW WOULD YOU RATE US AGAINST OUR COMPETITORS?

It's so difficult to be objective, and I really don't like to slight your competition.

IF PROBED FURTHER

Because I haven't flown with any of your major competitors it would be difficult for me to make any comparisons. However, from my research and talking to people who have flown with these airlines, it appears that XXX Airlines has the best reputation, in the way of safety record and providing customer care. XXX Airlines is recognised as being one of the worlds leading airlines.

DO YOU THINK XXX AIRLINES HAS A GOOD REPUTATION?

During my research into your airline, I did not come across any information that indicated a bad reputation, in fact quite the contrary, you seem to have a very good reputation.

WHAT HAVE YOU COME ACROSS THAT INDICATES A GOOD REPUTATION?

According to reports on airlines, XXX Airlines has surpassed many airlines on accreditations and awards which indicates and proves beyond all doubt that XXX Airlines has an excellent reputation and leads the way within the airline industry.

HOW DO YOU THINK WE CAN REMAIN SUCCESSFUL?

What you are doing now is working, so continue progressing the way you have done recently. I.e. increasing your variety of destinations, expanding your fleet of aircraft, and also introducing innovative technologies.

IS THERE ANY WAY IN WHICH YOU THINK WE CAN IMPROVE OUR SERVICE?

From my research into the airline industry, I have noticed that some airlines are introducing new trends. Such as massage therapy and beauty salons on board their planes. I think this is a good idea for XXX Airlines to consider, if it has not already been considered.

IS THERE ANYTHING YOU THINK WE DO BADLY?

I haven't come across anything to suggest that you are doing anything badly, in fact, quite the opposite. Plus I am sure you wouldn't enjoy your current success if you were doing anything really wrong and I wouldn't be applying to join you if that were the case.

WHAT DO YOU LOOK FOR IN AN AIRLINE?

I look for a good reputation in an active, creative and stimulating environment where I am limited only by my capabilities and where positive results are acknowledged. I believe XXX Airlines offers all of this and more.

HOW DO YOU RESEARCH THE AIRLINES YOU WISH TO WORK FOR?

First, I search the airlines website to learn more about the position, responsibilities and potential for growth, I then find out about their reputation, and visit the airline to meet the people who already work there and assess the overall environment.

HOW WOULD YOU COMPARE XXX AIRLINES TO THE OTHER AIRLINES YOU HAVE FLOWN WITH?

My experiences with each of the airlines I have flown with have all been good and I never had a problem or cause for complaint. However, an advantage of XXX Airlines is the diversity of the crew - I have never had such an excellent crew like on your flights. They really take care of all their passengers and do everything to make the flight as pleasant as possible. They are attentive, competent and very friendly and fun to talk to, and always smiling.

With XXX Airlines, I really felt like I was flying first class. The meal was outstanding, about the best you'll find anywhere - the seats were comfortable and the in-flight entertainment was very impressive, with a wide variety to choose from.

XXX Airlines really are a classy airline and deserve the 'airline of the year award'.

WHAT THREE TRENDS DO YOU SEE IN THE FUTURE FOR THE AIRLINE INDUSTRY?

Clearly the biggest trend is the move towards improved comfort - more room, fully reclining chairs. Also, better standards of service and seat-back entertainment.

THIS POSITION WILL INVOLVE RELOCATING, HOW WILL YOU ADJUST TO THE DIFFERENT LIFESTYLE?

I realise that this position involves transfers and I bore that in mind when I applied. I am fully aware of what to expect from the research I have done about any destination, and having visited the destination, I welcome the different lifestyle.

Or

I like England, but for this opportunity I am happy to relocate. I am fully aware of what to expect from the research I have done and would welcome the different lifestyle.

MISCELLANEOUS QUESTIONS

Miscellaneous

Salary History & Requirements

Haven't Experienced the Situation etc...

Questions for the Interviewer

TELL US ABOUT YOURSELF

There's so much I could tell you, but I want to be sure I focus on what's important to you. What specifically would you like to know?

I currently work as a freelance hairstylist and have worked in client facing roles for more than 8 years. I am looking for a change in my life and career direction and feel that a career as cabin crew would give me this.

Being a member of Cabin Crew is something I have always wanted to do and I feel that the qualities I possess and the skills and experience I have gained through my work experience will make me an excellent member of Cabin Crew and a valuable asset to any airline.

Being a member of cabin crew, I could use the customer and teamwork skills I have developed over the course of my career and be sufficiently challenged to develop further whilst learning from new people, processes and clients.

TELL US ABOUT A TIME WHEN YOUR SUPERIOR FOUND AN ERROR IN YOUR WORK, WHAT WAS THE OUTCOME OF THE WHOLE SITUATION?

I haven't made many errors in my work, owing to my attention to detail and the attention I pay to all aspects of each task. My errors came early in my career when I was training. Luckily, the errors were made on training heads, so I have learned from the errors and have not repeated them on actual clients.

WHAT HAVE YOU DONE THAT SHOWS INITIATIVE AND WILLINGNESS TO WORK/AT ANY HAIR SALON, WHAT DID YOU DO IN YOUR JOB THAT WAS NOT COVERED BY YOUR JOB DESCRIPTION?

To achieve peak performance, I always put in more effort than merely doing the job by the book. This comes naturally to me, as part of my work ethics. I am not happy with mediocre efforts because they lead to mediocre results.

At Any Hair Salon, to achieve goals and produce results, I sometimes performed various tasks that were not, strictly speaking, a part of my job. By doing more than required, I not only learn more, I also become more efficient and productive. If I'm able to do the task, instead of waiting for the job to be done, I simply do it.

For example...When I first began working at Any Hair Salon, the inventory system was outdated, and the storage room was very messy and disorganised, so I came in on my day off, cleaned up the mess, organised the store cupboards, and catalogued it all on the new inventory forms. Thereafter when orders arrived, it was easy to organise and therefore retrieve.

HOW WOULD I KNOW YOU WERE UNDER PRESSURE?

I disguise my pressure well; therefore you wouldn't know if I were under pressure.

WHAT QUESTION COULD I ASK YOU THAT WOULD REALLY INTIMIDATE YOU?

I can't think of any question that would intimidate me; this is probably the most intimidating question.

UNDER WHAT CIRCUMSTANCES DO YOU SEEK HELP?

I am aware of my own strengths but I am also prepared to ask for help from people with specialist knowledge.

If there is not much time and I need little help, I will seek assistance. Also, if I am confused, I will seek help – it's better to ask a dumb question than make a stupid mistake.

WHAT KIND OF THINGS DO YOU WORRY ABOUT/WHAT KEEPS YOU UP AT NIGHT?

I think worrying is pretty pointless – I prefer to take action and make changes. I have concerns, obviously – but for the most part I feel that I am in control of my life. However, areas that do concern me are meeting deadlines, reaching sales targets and getting supplies on time; just the normal stuff. But I wouldn't say that these things trouble me overly.

HOW WOULD YOU RATE ME AS AN INTERVIEWER?

First, I'd give you high marks for your people skills. You helped me feel at ease right away, which made it easier for me to answer the questions. I'd also rate you highly on the creativity of the questions and their thoroughness. By probing me as carefully as you have, you've given me a better opportunity to secure this position. You've given me a complete picture of what to expect at XXX Airlines, and it confirms my belief that this is where I want to work.

HAVE YOU BEEN COACHED IN INTERVIEW SKILLS?

Apart from studying interview books, No, I haven't.

WHAT IS AN ADEQUATE REWARD FOR YOUR EFFORTS?

My primary satisfaction and reward comes from a job well done and completed on time. The occasional good word from my boss or customer is always welcome, but not necessary.

HOW DO YOU FEEL ABOUT COMPANY RULES AND POLICIES?

I consider company rules, policies and procedures necessary for the efficient running of any business. They ensure that fairness, consistency and safety measures are applied across the board and that the right work environment is created and maintained. They help people make decisions and give them a sense of direction. My personal policy is always to observe the rules and make sure my colleagues observe them as well.

HAVE YOU EVER FELT CONSTRAINTS /HAVE YOU EVER HAD TO GO AGAINST THOSE TRADITIONS AND POLICIES TO REACH YOUR GOAL?

We all feel the constraints of some policies and procedures from time to time. However, to achieve uniformity and consistency and to ensure that relevant standards and regulations are followed, it is necessary to have those policies and procedures in place. It is always possible to cut corners and achieve the required results sooner or with less effort, but I have never taken the path of least resistance.

TO GET THE JOB DONE PEOPLE SOMETIMES HAVE TO BEND THE TRUTH. GIVE ME AN EXAMPLE WHEN YOU HAD TO DO THE SAME THING.

No I have never bent the truth and have always abided by company policies.

No matter how much you are probed, do not give in.

SOME PEOPLE FREQUENTLY TEND TO OVERSELL THE PRODUCT OR SERVICE TO MAKE A SALE, WHAT IS YOUR OPINION OF THAT TECHNIQUE?

I have never used the overselling technique. My philosophy in selling is that customers deserve unbiased and honest advice on products and services. Anyone who misleads the buyers creates a very negative image for the company and himself, and loses credibility, which is one of the most precious attributes in business.

HAVE YOU STRETCHED THE TRUTH TODAY TO GAIN A FAVOURABLE OUTCOME?

No, I haven't tried to be someone I am not, because I wouldn't want to get the job that way. To win that way would be such a short term gain because eventually I would be found out.

IF YOU COULD BE ANYONE, WHO WOULD YOU LIKE TO BE?

Generally, I'd say I'm pretty happy with who I am and what I've done with my life. I have no desire to be anyone other than myself.

No matter how much you are probed, do not give in.

IF YOU COULD DO ANYTHING, WHAT WOULD YOU DO?

I am applying for this job because this is what I want to do, therefore I would continue with what I am doing now.

SO YOU WOULDN'T CHOOSE TO BE A MILLIONAIRE AND OPT FOR AN EASY LIFE?

I don't have any desire for an easy life. Nothing worth having in life comes easily. I suppose an easy life would be nice for a while, but then I would become restless. For now, I'm interested in achievement, accomplishment, and seeing just how much I can do with the talent and intelligence I have. My career remains my first priority.

IF YOU WERE AN ANIMAL, WHICH WOULD YOU BE AND WHY?

I would be a horse. Horses are friendly and outgoing, and they like to be around others. They have boundless energy and ambition and enjoy being physically active.

DO YOU HAVE ANY FEAR THAT WOULD DETER YOU TRAVELLING BY AIR?

None at all; I love to fly.

SALARY HISTORY AND REQUIREMENTS

WHAT IS YOUR SALARY HISTORY/WHAT IS YOUR CURRENT SALARY?

My salary history has followed a steady upward path. I started out earning £280 per month as a receptionist, which later rose to £360. As a junior hairstylist my salary rose to £600, and as a senior, my salary was £720 per month. I feel that these increases reflect my performance and the extra responsibilities I assumed during the course of my employment.

Working Freelance, my personal salary changes week by week depending on work flow, however, to give you an example, last year my personal salary came to £10,500.

YOU KNOW WHAT WE'RE PREPARED TO PAY FOR THIS POSITION, WOULD YOU BE PREPARED TO ACCEPT THIS FIGURE?

Salary is not the most important thing as far as I'm concerned. I'm more concerned about finding the right job and the right employer. I'm sure the salary wouldn't prove to be a problem.

WHAT DO YOU THINK YOU SHOULD BE EARNING IN 5 YEARS?

I hope that my pay will reflect my contribution to the organisation, but the most important thing for me is job satisfaction and compatibility with the team I work with and the company I work for.

HAVEN'T EXPERIENCED THE SITUATION, ETC.

If you are really stuck and cannot answer a question, or if you haven't experienced a situation that you are being asked about, then it is best to say so. A quietly confident admission is more impressive than trying to bluff your way through or saying nothing at all.

- I am sorry, but that isn't an area I am familiar with at present, so I can't really give you any details on that.
- I am sorry, but I haven't come across that particular term before, would you mind clarifying it for me.
- That is a new area for me, so I am afraid I can't really answer that, but I enjoy acquiring new knowledge and I do learn quickly.
- Sorry, I've never been in that situation. I could imagine my response if you like.
- Sorry, I can't remember ever being in that situation, but I did face something slightly similar that I could discuss.
- I've never been in that situation, but assuming I was successful and working for you, I think I'd handle it like this ____.
- That's a tough question; I need time to think about my answer. Can we come back to it later?
- That's an interesting question, may I have a moment or two to collect my thoughts.
- There is quite a lot I could say about that, can you bear with me while I think about that for a minute.
- I am not sure where I should start with that, please would you give me a little bit more of an explanation.
- Sorry, I'm not sure I understand, could you repeat the question please.

QUESTIONS FOR THE INTERVIEWERS

The questions you ask the recruiters can say a lot about you and what you know about the airline and the position itself. Therefore, it is a good idea to prepare one or two intelligent questions in advance.

Your list of questions needs to follow these guidelines:

- Don't ask questions that could be easily answered through your own research.
- Ask questions which demonstrate a genuine interest in and knowledge of the Airline and the position.
- Your questions should also demonstrate that you know just that little bit more than is required. Sort of bonus features if they take you on.

Below are some good examples of the sorts of questions you could ask.

- How did you get into this industry/Why did you choose to work for XXX Airlines?
- What is it about this Airline that keeps you here?
- It sounds as if you really enjoy working here, what have you enjoyed most about working for XXX Airlines?
- Is there anything else I need to do to maximise my chances of getting this job?
- How soon after being successful would I begin training?
- I am looking for a long term career with you and if I am lucky enough to be offered the position, what opportunities would there be for promotion in the future?

- Do you have any reservations about my ability to do this job/What do you foresee as possible obstacles or problems I might have?
  This is a good question to ask as the interviewer will disclose their concerns. You can then follow up to reassure the interviewer... You could say something like 'Thank you. That has been very helpful, perhaps then it would be helpful for you to know that _____.'

NO QUESTIONS.

I did have plenty of questions, but we've covered them all during our discussions. I was particularly interested in ___, but we've dealt with that thoroughly.

I had many questions, but you've answered them all you've been so helpful. I'm even more excited about this opportunity than when I applied.

INDEX

BACKGROUND

Personal details

Outside interests

Education and training

School

Further Education and Training

Current and Future Development

General

Work experience and employment history

Previous Employers

Co-workers

Present Employment

Professional knowledge and experience

SKILLS & ABILITIES

Personal traits and skills

My Views

Communication/Interpersonal skills

Decision making

GENERAL MOTIVES & PERCEPTIONS

Knowledge and Suitability for the job

Cabin Crew

General perceptions

PERCEPTIONS ABOUT CUSTOMER SERVICE

PERCEPTIONS ABOUT TEAMWORK & WORKING RELATIONSHIPS

HYPOTHETICAL QUESTIONS

TECHNICAL QUESTIONS

Career goals and future progression

About the Airline

MISCELLANEOUS QUESTIONS

Salary history and requirements

NOTES

Smile, Be confident

NOTES

NOTES

NOTES

NOTES